HEALTH INTUITION

"*Health Intuition* is a practical handbook for achieving greater well-being and true balance by expanding that inner wisdom known as intuition. With many simple and effective suggestions and applications, Karen Grace Kassy skillfully guides you through the principles of healing yourself and others."

—Sonia Choquette, Ph.D.
Author of *The Psychic Pathway, Your Heart's Desire, The Wise Child*, and *True Balance*

"*Health Intuition* is beautifully written. Karen Grace Kassy's work is a foundational construction in the emerging field of energy medicine education. Her insights will shed light into the frontier in the study on intuition and energy medicine. This work will become a classic in the field."

—Douglass Capagrossi, Ph.D.
President of Greenwich University
Professional consultant in education and training

"Karen Grace Kassy is the real thing. She is a natural teacher with genuine intuitive skills. Her work is filled with integrity, compassion, and non-judgment, and she provides . . . real-life examples and doable exercises that bring theory into practice. Kassy is able to take right-brained material and present it in an organized and systematic way. You walk away from her book with skills that you can develop and use in daily life as well as in a therapeutic practice. I highly recommend this book for anyone wanting to learn how to tap into their inner knowing."

—Adele R. McDowell, Ph.D.
Founder and director of The Greenheart Center

"Karen Grace Kassy charts a clear and concise road map for rediscovering and reawakening our own inherent intuitive abilities. This book is an essential resource for anyone interested in expanding their awareness or deep personal growth and transformation."

—Jan Hendryx, D.O.
Medical director, Hendryx Wellness Centre
Bradford, Pennsylvania

HEALTH INTUITION

A SIMPLE GUIDE TO GREATER WELL-BEING

BY KAREN GRACE KASSY

TRANSITIONS
BOOKPLACE

HAZELDEN®

INFORMATION & EDUCATIONAL SERVICES

Hazelden
Center City, Minnesota 55012-0176
1-800-328-0094
1-651-213-4590 (Fax)
www.hazelden.org

Health Intuition[sm] and Health Intuitive[sm] are service marks
owned by Karen Kassy. In order to facilitate reading the SM symbol
does not appear in each instance these terms are used; however,
this in no way affects Karen Kassy's ownership of the service marks.

Author's note
The material in this book is not intended to replace competent medical treatment or psychotherapy, diagnose illness, or
prescribe medical treatment. If you, your clients, or patients
have physical, mental, emotional, and/or spiritual problems,
please seek the help of a competent health care professional.
Every story in this book is true; however, each has been
edited for clarity. Names, locations, and other identifying
information have been changed to protect confidentiality.

Library of Congress Cataloging-in-Publication Data
Kassy, Karen Grace.
    Health intuition : a simple guide to greater well-being / by Karen Grace
Kassy ; [foreword by Caroline Myss].
        p. cm.
    Includes bibliographical references and index.
    ISBN 1-56838-563-3 (hardcover)
    1. Healing. 2. Intuition (Psychology) 3. Mental healing. 4. Mind and
body therapies. 5. Self-care, Health. I. Title.

RZ999.K28 2000
616.8'52—dc21   00-040994

04 03 02 01 00   6 5 4 3 2

Cover design by David Spohn
Interior design by Nora Koch / Gravel Pit Publications
Typesetting by Universal Press

DEDICATION

For Patrick, Joseph, and Caroline

CONTENTS

CONTENTS

FOREWORD

Since the fall of 1984, when I first began working with the fields of intuition and health as a medical intuitive, I have seen an incredible increase of interest in the coupling of these two areas. We ask the questions "Why am I sick?" and "What can I do about it?" It seems that we've reached a time when we are now ready and willing to rely on our deepest inner knowing for answers. On the other hand, we are deeply logical and analytical creatures—how do we combine these two seemingly disparate worlds? Pursuing this quest and offering a plan to help people create this balance of intuition and intellect is the rich goal of this remarkable book by Karen Grace Kassy, M.S.

Karen is someone whom I've watched develop for quite some time. We first met several years ago, following an interesting turn of events. Karen was employed by my tape publisher. She had heard my audio program *Why People Don't Heal.* Fascinated, she wanted to learn more. The day before she was to come to one of my workshops, she picked out a gift for me, some musical tapes designed to aid healing. We never did meet that day. For the first time in fourteen years, I had to cancel a speaking engagement—I was sick. Karen later sent the tapes to me, with a note, "I knew you were a medical intuitive and probably know why everyone is sick and therefore how to be incredibly healthy yourself, but for some reason, these tapes on healing really drew me. Then you ended up sick. Isn't that a funny coincidence?"

Karen has come a long way from attributing meaningful events to "funny coincidence." A few months after we eventually met, she picked me up at the airport to take me to a taping. With some trepidation, she confessed, "I know all of your friends probably think they are becoming medically intuitive, but I really think it's happening to me. I've been researching the field and practicing. I seem to possess this ability." I quickly reassured her that *none* of my friends wanted to be medically intuitive, but that I did think it was something that was happening to her. And, with the publication of her book, it's something that can happen for you too.

Karen's background and bachelor's degree are in business, and, with that, she brings a down-to-earth approach that oftentimes is missing in this field. She has also intelligently researched the field of intuition, earning a master's degree in energy medicine and intuition. She calls herself a "health intuitive" instead of "medical intuitive," to place greater emphasis on the goal of health. She is an accurate health intuitive, with a physician-verified ability and health care practitioners who refer patients to her regularly. Early in her studies, I strongly recommended she follow a similar path to mine: completing an internship with a physician. Karen has a fantastic passion for learning. She not only interned with a physician, she took my suggestion to another level and worked with health care practitioners from many phases of complementary medicine. With this broader perspective, Karen continues to take her field and understanding to new levels.

After developing a simple and accurate method of intuitive diagnosis, she began teaching her technique to audiences worldwide—with great success. She teaches that intuition is not a substitute for health care, and I heartily agree. Rather, in our fast-paced era of information overload, it is a way to clarify information and offer a new perspective. As we are faced with more choices in holistic health care, intuition offers a common ground with which to synthesize approaches—taking the best of the best to save the patient and health care system time and money.

Karen is a wonderful communicator, both in spoken and written word. Despite there being more books available on health and intuition than ever before, her book stands out for its easy-to-follow, organized, and straightforward approach. Simply put, her method works.

Through my work as a medical intuitive, I realize that health is about learning lessons. To this end, recognizing what "unfinished business" each of us has in terms of patterns, issues, and problems is key to resolving health issues and becoming more intuitive. In section 1 of this book, Karen has identified a series of common issues that she sees while working with clients as a health intuitive. Unlike many self-help books today, she provides practical solutions—not just theories—that can improve health and well-being. It is crucial for each of us to investigate these mental, spiritual, and emotional issues and to recognize which ones affect us. In each chapter, Karen provides a self-test of questions and key indicators that will help you discover, and work to transcend, the issues in your life.

In my own work, I meet so many people who want to learn intuitive diagnosis. I have also met many people who attest that they have this ability, only to be disappointed by their lack of accuracy or integrity. Bringing a simple and effective method of intuitive diagnosis into the public domain (in section 2) may raise concerns that this information will be misused. Because Karen addresses this drawback and others with compassion and integrity, I feel that the door has been opened for us to safely explore our birthright of intuition.

Health Intuition: A Simple Guide to Greater Well-Being is the finest book I have read on developing an awareness of the intimate connection between one's intuition and the four levels of health (physical, mental, emotional, and spiritual) and well-being. This delicious guide is not a one-size-fits-all intuitive program—thank goodness—rather, it is an empowering resource that can aid each of us in learning to listen to our inner voice and improving health and well-being.

—Caroline Myss, Ph.D.

INTRODUCTION

What is health intuition? It is a verifiable skill that uses the inner sense that we all have to lead to improved health and well-being. Health intuition can be used by health care practitioners to help their clients and patients and by ordinary people who want to understand why they are not at maximum health and what they can do physically, mentally, emotionally, and spiritually to improve their lives. Whether you're a person in a health-related field, or someone who is interested in your own and your loved ones' health and healing, following the steps in this book can help you develop your intuition to learn the root causes of illness and what to do to shift into greater health and well-being.

Until the 1990s, it was rare to hear of using intuition to diagnose health problems in our modern culture. However, this decade marked a change in climate from a traditional medical model toward a more inclusive system of complementary/alternative healing. In 1997, a follow-up study[1] published in the *Journal of the American Medical Association* stated that Americans had spent $10 billion out-of-pocket on alternative methods of healing in a single year—a trend that showed far more spending than in previous times. Why the shift? As patients and clinicians move toward a more open-minded model of holistic healing, they are more likely to try new modalities of treatment and diagnosis. Whereas several years ago, complementary approaches such as acupuncture, homeopathy, and herbalism would not have been discussed, today they are offered in many clinical settings. Americans seem to find value in the various complementary modalities of care offered and they show it by spending their own money for treatments that aren't covered by insurance.

Within this more holistic atmosphere, science is taking a new look at age-old healing traditions that humans have relied on for thousands of years, such as herbalism, massage, homeopathy, acupuncture, and intuition. How often is intuition used in a medical setting? Even though the climate is more open-minded and intuition has lost its stigma in some circles, clinicians often are reluctant to talk about their abilities; however, for my master's degree thesis, I surveyed a group of people who use their intuition to accurately diagnose health problems. Eighty-nine percent of the respondents were from a medical background, including physicians and nurses.

I work as a health intuitive. This means that I use my intuitive skills to survey the health of a client. I focus in on two pieces of information: a client's name and age. Knowing nothing else, I am able to discern the person's physical, mental, emotional, and spiritual health with up to 90 percent average accuracy (physician verified). I do this long-distance, over the telephone. Although this may seem amazing to you (it is to me!), it also gives rise to skepticism: How can this work? Is this a real thing? In the following pages, I will tell you how it works, and you can decide for yourself whether health intuition is indeed real.

The material in this book comes from three places: my intuitive evaluations (readings) of clients, my teaching work with students, and my research. I have accurately evaluated countless clients, providing them with insight into how they can improve their health and well-being. Over the years, I have noticed certain patterns, problems, and issues that keep people from living truly fulfilling lives. But no one wants to read a self-help book that says, "Here are ninety-seven things that are wrong with you. The end." And my clients don't want a reading that is a list of their problems—they want solutions.

In section 1 of this book, I describe common physical, mental, emotional, and spiritual patterns I see in many of my clients. They are people just like you, who are working to make their lives better. They come from all walks of life: mothers, fathers, daughters, sons, car mechanics, doctors, secretaries, executives, and so on. Some of them are in poor physical health: AIDS, cancer, diabetes, so tired they cannot get out of bed, and so on. Others sense that there is more to their physical problems (or those of their patients and clients, in the case of health care professionals) than is readily discernible. They want to know where the health problem started, what was the cause, and what is happening on the emotional, mental, and spiritual levels that contributes to their lack of health. Some of my clients are in good health, but curious about my work. Whatever reasons are behind someone's decision to seek a consultation with me, we work together to come up with practical and workable solutions to his or her problems.

After noticing how many of these solutions worked for a wide range of people, I started teaching others about them in a workshop format. Even without the benefit of a personal reading with me, my students were able to successfully apply these concepts to problems and issues they were facing. These same solutions are contained in section 1—solutions that you can apply to transcend and change. As you work on your issues, you may find, like my clients and students, that your health and well-being improve.

Throughout this book, I have included case studies and stories, from workshops I have taught and readings I have conducted, illustrating universal concepts that can improve health. I hope you will learn from this information, just as I have, and incorporate the concepts that resonate for you in your life.

With an improvement in your health and well-being, you may notice something else: an interest in how to come up with this information yourself. In section 2, I teach you my health intuition method. I have taught this process to thousands of people through my workshops. You will learn to listen to yourself and to develop the skill I believe everyone has: intuition. Let me assure you, it does take some practice. If you wanted to be a good piano player, how would you go about it? Perhaps get a book, take lessons, set the intention or goal, and practice, practice, practice. Intuition is no different—it requires the same intention and practice you would give to any new skill you wanted to learn. With this in mind, I have included intuitive exercises in this book, which will show you how I "tune in" and how you can learn to also. I have taught the health intuition method to everyone from my mom (!) to bodyworkers, alternative health care practitioners, R.N.s, M.D.s, and Ph.D.s. I am convinced that this is a skill that can be learned and used for greater insights into our own lives, as well as those of our loved ones and clients, and this book will teach you how. Remember: set the intention and practice, practice, practice.

My clients and students are excited and grateful for the insights given to them through health intuition, and who wouldn't be? You can derive these same benefits from reading and practicing what you learn in this book. Like my clients and students, you will find ways to enhance your health and well-being through learning to listen to yourself.

SECTION I

CHAPTER 1

My Work, Myself

Students and clients are always interested in how I started in this unusual profession as a health intuitive. Like everything else in my life, it just seemed to happen. Unlike everything else in my life, it came about with ease and grace, instead of the usual planning and ambitious attempt to control and manipulate the future. Sometimes I use the phrase *by accident* to describe the extraordinary events that happen to me all the time now. It's another term for the beautiful *synchronicities* (Carl Jung's term for meaningful coincidences) that constantly have arisen since this path began for me years ago. I truly believe, and teach my students and clients, that this can happen for you: a healthy life, full of meaningful happenings, that brings you with ease to the place you want to be. A place of passion, synchronicity, trust, and inner knowing. This is the place of health intuition, where life makes sense and you can work toward health.

MY EARLY YEARS

I grew up in the second-most Republican county in America. I'm surprised it's not called "Conservative-ville." Looking back, I can see that I was always intuitive. I believe everyone is as a child, whether they are conscious of it or not. My Catholic family teased me, calling intuition my "direct pipeline to God." I would use the pipeline to find missing items for them. Although my family accepted my ability within a religious context, there was no other talk about it. I wasn't chastised for "knowing things," but it was silently understood that this wasn't something to be talked about out in public, especially not in our conservative community. Growing up, I don't remember knowing anyone who possessed intuitive abilities, but life was full of other things to do, so it wasn't a big concern for me.

On weekends, my dad sometimes took me to the horse races. With nothing better to do than wish I had a horse, I would "feel" which horse would win; more often than not, I was correct.

One day, we took my friend Laura to the track with us. To relieve her quickly developing boredom, I decided to teach her my system. That day Laura and I picked seven winners in a row, came in second in the eighth race, and won again in the ninth. (No betting—we were only ten years old.) In explaining our astonishing results to my father, Laura said, "You just tune in and see how the horses feel, and then you know who will win."

She was my first student. Years later, I follow the same protocol to intuitively tune in while doing health readings, and my students follow it too.

In my teen years, I turned away from my intuitive side. I felt frustrated by my perception that the Catholic religion did not seem to hold any answers for me. I left my connections to the divine, intuition, and Catholicism behind, because I believed that they were inseparable from one another. I also had fears surrounding my second sight. When I knew something bad would happen, and it did, my young mind wondered, *Did I cause that?* I did not have access to people, books, or resources that would show me otherwise. Years later, as I work with people who turned off their intuition during adolescence because of fear and misunderstanding, I can empathize and help them overcome these blocks because of my own experiences.

In my thirties, my intuition reawakened. I met an intuitive at a conference, and we decided to share a meal. I was surprised at how normal she seemed. She talked easily about everyday things and did *not* dress like a fortune teller. I found her ordinary behavior (and mode of dress) reassuring. I remember being surprised that she ordered a meat dish for dinner. From the perspective of my conservative upbringing, I assumed she would be a vegetarian. In the middle of ordering, she turned to the waitress and said: "Honey, get that left ovary checked. That cyst is growing. I'll have mashed potatoes and lemon pie." The waitress, unfazed, said, "You're right. I've been meaning to get that looked at."

I was speechless, but my mind was racing. *Fascinating! I wonder how she does that? I wonder if I could do it?*

I returned home, filled with curiosity. I wondered how someone who seemed so "normal" could have such power. How could a total stranger know another person's medical condition? I enjoy research—my mind combines a love of learning with a strong bent for detective work—and I had access to a wealth of resources. My employer recorded and produced tapes on spirituality, health and healing, meditation, psychology, and even intuition. Working at "Spirituality Central" gave me access not only to tapes but to books and people as well. As head of the conference division, I was able to travel and talk with leading authors and speakers in their fields. Additionally, one of my co-workers, George, began to answer my questions and mentor me in areas of spiritual wisdom.

When I mentioned my newfound interest in the intuitive realm to George, he told me that he knew how a person could become medically intuitive (like the woman I had met at the conference). He suggested that I picture a computer in my mind. If I wanted medical information on someone, I should type in their name and age (simply as a focal point), and wait for an answer. I thanked him for the idea, but his suggestion seemed too simple to be valid. The skeptic in me totally discounted his idea as being too easy. I assumed that the hard way is always the best way.

Later that week, I received a phone call from Jim, a vendor. Only twenty-six years old and extremely accomplished, he was head of a major corporation's conference department. I enjoyed our conversations, as he was full of fun and very open to discussing unusual ideas. As we spoke, I started getting an overwhelming impression that had nothing to do with our conversation. The image in my mind's eye was one of the Greek god Atlas, with a big globe on his shoulders. I pushed the visual imprint away, but it kept coming back, distracting me from the conversation.

Finally, I said, "Jim, I think I'm getting an intuitive impression about your health. May I share it with you?"

"Sure."

"I see you like Atlas, with a big globe on your shoulders. Do you have shoulder problems?"

"Bursitis in both," he replied. I was so startled that I didn't respond. "Karen," he said, "can your intuition tell me what to do about this?"

"I don't know," I replied.

"Well, tune in!" I did as George had suggested: I pictured a computer in my mind's eye. I typed in Jim's name and age. Up popped a body with two red dots, one on each shoulder. I clicked on my imaginary magnification tool and dragged it to the shoulder area. Printed on my imaginary computer screen was an explanation. I read it out loud to Jim:

"It seems that you are the type of person who has trouble delegating. You're the most responsible person you know, and you do it all. Also, you may want things done your way and have trouble allowing others to use their own approaches. Could you possibly delegate and work on being more allowing toward others?" I asked.

"I'd rather get cortisone shots in my shoulders every day than delegate or allow," he said.

Jim's "reading" taught me my first two lessons about health intuition: (1) ask before offering intuitive advice, and (2) when you deliver the information, don't be attached to what the recipient does with it. Not being attached to the outcome has proved to be a reliable method of dealing with clients and with everyone else in my daily life as well. I have learned that if I release my expectations, I am not disappointed or de-energized when people go their way, not my way. Every reading has at least one lesson in it for me. These were the first of many.

As time went on, encouraged by friends and later by friends of friends, I began to do more readings. I learned that there is a mind-body connection to every physical manifestation of disease. (Later, I would see the role spirit plays in this association.) Each time I tuned in intuitively, I wondered if "it" would work. It always did. But still, I considered my intuition a neat party trick I had discovered and did not take it very seriously. Despite the accuracy of my readings, I was still skeptical. I could not yet believe that something so intangible could be real.

HOW I BEGAN TO LEARN AND TEACH HEALTH INTUITION

One day, having completed a reading for a friend of a friend, I got a call from her holistic physician in New England. *Now you're busted,* I thought. *You're a big fraud, and this doctor is going to tell you what harm you've caused.* The opposite occurred. Dr. Sharon Black assured me that I was talented and told me that she wanted to work with me. She gave me the names and ages of twenty of her patients and asked me to do readings for them. I procrastinated endlessly—my first case of stage fright. I was plagued with skepticism, doubt, and a supreme lack of confidence. Finally, I tuned in, got the information, and sent off the readings.

A month went by with no call from Dr. Black. Two months, no call. After three months, I worked up the courage to leave her a voice mail message. A few days later, I received a beautiful card in the mail from her. She said that the readings were very accurate, apologized for her slow response (the result of a busy schedule), and promised to call the following Saturday night with feedback.

I nervously awaited the call, with forty sheets of typewritten readings and a yellow highlighter to mark the occasional hit. At the end of our hour-long conversation, I was shaking as I hung up the phone. The forty pages were almost completely covered in yellow. The doctor's validation of my readings hit home—this was a real ability. I had figured out how to do it, and it worked.

Since then, I have worked with hundreds of clients and health care practitioners. Using only a person's name and age as input, I can discern physical, mental, emotional, and spiritual health with an average accuracy of 80 to 90 percent (physician verified). I do this work long-distance, usually over the phone, but fax, mail, and E-mail also work as methods of communication. My client base is worldwide and covers all ages. My youngest client is a two-year-old girl in Ireland; the oldest is a woman in her eighties in Canada.

Age and distance seem to be no barrier to my intuition, although I admit that the first time I did a reading for someone across an ocean, I wondered if my intuition would work. I gave it a try, and it did. Through experience and practice, I have built confidence. When some new challenge for my intuition comes along, I relax and remember all of the times intuition has helped me (and others), be it with health problems or finding a parking place in a crowded lot. After all of these years, I still go with the basics, and of course, I practice and hold a clear intention.

When I began learning to be a health intuitive, I didn't realize how solitary my path would be. Sure, there were books, tapes, workshops, and even an occasional contact with an intuitive to help light the way. However, I deeply wanted someone to hold my hand through this most frightening time in my life. Like many other people, I had turned away from my intuition in my teen years, in part because I did not know what to do with my impressions. I had no resources to deal with them, and I was afraid. Now, I was in my thirties, trying to avoid the concerns and problems of the past, but I needed reassurance. I wanted a mentor who could be with me *every* step of the way. There was no one.

I can look back now and see the purpose of my solitary journey. I wished then that I could suddenly have perfectly developed intuition—perhaps be struck by lightning (unharmed, of course, except for enhanced intuitive powers). Now I believe I know why I needed to learn each piece: I am meant to teach intuition. If I didn't know how I got here, how could I show anyone else the path? I needed to figure it out myself, step-by-step, and experience a range of challenges, so that I could identify with every student and be able to answer his or her questions.

What follows in this book is the program that I discovered on my intuitive path. It is by no means new—I believe that throughout history, many people have come up with similar ideas. When I attend workshops, listen to tapes, or read books on intuition, I often find parallels to my work in ancient traditions, such as healing, shamanism, and other forms of spirituality. As I learn more about the historical background of intuitive practice and development in other cultures and among individuals, I find many similarities with my own work. At the Healing Touch Conference in 1998, Brugh Joy, M.D., spoke about how in the past, *sensitives* (an old-fashioned word for *intuitives*) used a nonphysical entry point, and an exit point, when reading someone's energy.[1] I use an invocation to begin my work and a simple ritual to finish.

There are probably many teachers who have similar ideas. This does not bother me a bit. After all, if something is truth, it is perceived—and can be taught—in many different ways. This is the piece of truth that I have found and the way I teach it. I follow the KISS (Keep It Simple, Sweetheart) approach: it works, it's uncomplicated, and I believe that, with practice, anyone can master it. Some may go further with it than others, depending on their desire, ability, and other skills. It is not a competition. You get out of it what you invest. What intuitive ability comes will be right for you. Avoid comparing yourself with others; give the gift of focus and attention to yourself.

CHAPTER 2

What Is Intuition?

Over the years, I have researched intuition through books, tapes, workshops, and personal experience. There is a wealth of information and scientific study available on something that is considered "not real" by many people. For example, Russell Targ and Keith Harary[1] conducted groundbreaking work starting in the 1970s at Stanford University. More recently, Dr. Valerie Hunt[2] of UCLA has documented some interesting phenomena. A good overall view of the modern technology and research in this area can be found in Michael Talbot's *Holographic Universe.*[3]

To see how many people have experienced this "unreal" phenomenon, I often ask people in my workshops to describe one intuitive occurrence they have experienced. Here is a small sampling of the answers I receive:

"The phone rang, and I knew who it would be."

"I have precognitive and predictive dreams. When I awaken, they come true within a matter of days."

"I am a health professional and often have intuitive feelings about my patients. More often than not, although they seem to come completely out of left field, they are correct."

"I know when unexpected guests will drop by, so I'm never unprepared."

"I'll be thinking about someone I haven't thought of or seen in years. The very next day, I'll run into that person."

"If I can't find something, I close my eyes, imagine where it is, and see it. When I look in the place I visualized, there it is."

"Meaningful coincidences, which I call synchronicities, happen all the time. For example, I'll need something for my home. I'll happen to drive by a garage sale, stop, and there it is. Or I'll pick up the phone to call my mother, and she's on the line calling me—the phone didn't even ring!"

"As a child, I knew when someone was going to die."

"If I concentrate really hard, I can find lost items for friends."

"I knew who was on the phone the other day before I answered it—and I don't have caller ID."

"Once in a while, I'll have a dream about someone or something strange, and it comes true."

"If I picture the perfect parking spot in my mind, it is always there waiting for me, no matter how busy or crowded the streets are."

"As a health care practitioner, I seem to sense when something is wrong with my patients. I call them to check, and they are amazed, because some health concern had just arisen. This happens whether I have seen them recently or several years ago."

Juanita, a student from New York City, said: "I can't list just one. I do it at the grocery store (What do I need? How much will my groceries be?); at the gas pump (What will it cost to fill up my tank?); in traffic (What is the best route? Where is the best parking spot?); and on and on."

I loved Juanita's answer. She exemplifies someone who practices constantly, on everyday things, which hones her sense and confidence in her inner knowing. She listens to herself all the time. As you begin to listen to and trust your inner voice, intuitive occurrences happen with greater frequency. Think of it as a new friendship that you have to cultivate and give attention and respect to. Intuition will blossom into the best relationship you'll ever have—the one with yourself. You've already taken the first step on this journey by picking up this book.

I also ask my students, "What are some different words for *intuition*?" Here is a small sampling of the terms they suggest: *psychic, ESP (extrasensory perception), insight, impression, a funny feeling, hunch, vibe, premonition, gut instinct, channel, prophecy, revelation, medium, foreshadowing, foreboding, dream, witchcraft, second sight, voodoo, hit (or miss),* and *sixth sense.* As you can see, there are a lot of words for an ability that in the Western Hemisphere is considered unprovable by some people. One of the reasons I bring all these terms to your attention is so you have the right words to communicate your intuitive impressions. For example, my father is very scientific. He prefers the term *ESP*. When I use this term with him, I gain credibility, and he listens. A friend of mine is a fundamentalist Christian. He theorizes that my intuition may be the work of the devil and is not interested in my impressions unless I tell him that I had a dream about him. He has dreams, too, so he can relate. Using the benign term *dream* helps me get my intuitive impressions across without upsetting him. The right words can help you get your message across too.

Many words and experiences can be used to illustrate intuition, but coming up with a definition is tricky. I have heard and read some technical and scientific explanations; however, my favorite is this one: "Intuition is knowing something without knowing how you know it." When something comes to us out of the blue—something about which we have had no previous knowledge—and it turns out to be true, how do we explain it? I do not come from a medical background, and yet I am able to diagnose people with a high rate of accuracy. Most of us have crossed paths with someone who seems to have a degree of psychic ability. It may not be tangible or always scientifically provable (although there is a great deal of scientific research available), but for thousands of years, people have relied on this sixth sense, no matter what words are used to define, describe, and explain it.

Even the practitioners of modern medicine are still striving for more tools to aid in diagnosis. Would intuition be a helpful adjunct? Dr. C. Norman Shealy states:

> Although we physicians are generally about 80% accurate in our primary diagnostic attempts, we are frustrated in determining the *exact* diagnoses for a variety of illnesses. Furthermore, many of the diagnostic tests carry a significant risk of damage to the patient. In instances such as these, it seems most obvious that the opinion of two or three talented intuitives could help us avoid risky diagnostic tests and help both physician and patient.[4]

WHY DEVELOP INTUITION?

One reason to develop intuition is to improve health and well-being. My clients, students, and I have reaped other benefits as well from practicing our intuitive skills. In our society, we are overwhelmed by information. Recently, I heard this astonishing statistic on the radio: During the 1950s, the knowledge in our world doubled every fifty years; now it doubles every two years. How do we keep up with what we need to know? Where should we give our attention? Intuition can help: it can draw you to what you need to see or learn. I use it in business to help me weed through resumés, reports, and E-mail. I rely on it to quickly and accurately assess people's characters, especially in interviewing and hiring job candidates, as well as to appraise compatibility for possible friendships and romantic relationships. Decision making can be enhanced through intuition: What is the bottom line here? This situation is confusing—what do I need to know? Intuition not only augments decision making, it can help you gain confidence and, consequently, the courage to act.

Intuition can help you improve relationships. Communication is important and often complicated in interpersonal interactions. In a compassionate way, intuition can cut to the heart of the matter, helping you understand barely perceptible and subtle signals. Recently, I did a reading for a man from Texas. Ben is a successful businessman, working on incorporating spirituality into his work and life. In his reading, I said, "Start relating heart-to-heart, every time. Picture the person you want to communicate with, and see or feel your heart connecting to his or hers before you ever open your mouth. Be silent if you need to before speaking in social situations, work, or relationships. This is the key you are looking for."

As often happens when I give a reading, Ben found the words very validating. In the week before our session, he had stumbled onto this same concept. A longtime friend of his, who had a fundamentalist viewpoint, was hard to talk to—not only for Ben, but also for many of the friends in their group. Ben took a deep breath and imagined his heart connecting to his friend's. As they spoke, everyone was amazed. For the first time in years, someone was actually communicating with this person, and he was not getting upset, but instead was having a reasonable, relevant conversation. It was an incredible breakthrough and led to an improved relationship for all who witnessed it.

Using intuition in relation to yourself can help you be more aware of your needs, such as needs for sleep, food, and health. As you learn to appropriately satisfy these needs, you experience less frustration. Also, by trusting yourself enough to listen to your inner voice, you can find your true calling by becoming aware of what your passion is, what gives you meaning in life, what your goals are, and what you aspire to be and do. In short, intuition helps you find yourself. I venture to guess that there is almost no one who has not asked the question "Who am I?" With intuition, you are that much closer to finding your true essence. Once you are congruent with the self and have that kind of trust, there is less internal conflict. Fear is not such an issue, because you trust your instincts to warn you of any danger and tell you what you need to know. I have seen this congruence with the self, and the subsequent lessening of fears, lead to greater health and well-being.

HEALTH INTUITION

I call what I do "health intuition." Some people call it "medical intuition," but I believe that the term *health* better connotes a process, a goal, or an outcome. It encompasses the pieces of the puzzle that contribute to health—physical, mental, emotional, and spiritual— whereas the term *medical* does not always take these four areas into account. Why did I focus on health and not some other kind of specialty? As a child, my father often said to me, "If you don't have your health, you don't have anything. All the money in the world is meaningless if you don't feel healthy." Those words have stuck with me. My belief is that if we feel that we are at our best, we can then pursue life to its fullest. That's what I want for myself, and that's what many of my clients and students want for themselves. Sharing with others how to discover their own (or their patients') cause of lack of health and what to do about it opens to everyone the possibility of attaining their full potential.

When I started researching and practicing intuition, I was surprised to learn that there are four levels of health and a mind-body-spirit connection. I knew that stress contributed to illness, but I was amazed to intuitively see a basis for health problems in the mental, emotional, or spiritual realms before manifesting physically. I am often stunned at the information I receive: facts that I am completely unaware of beforehand, or even information that is the opposite of what I believe. Time and again, my insights are later validated by clients, health care professionals, books, and scientific research.

All four levels of health are included in a health intuition reading: physical, mental, emotional, and spiritual. I look at the past, present, and potential future. During the reading, I cover what's physically wrong with my client, but the content of the readings seems to be about 5 to 10 percent physical in nature. The rest of the information is primarily focused on what underlies this level: the emotional, spiritual, and mental insights behind the physical issues. When I first started this work, I thought I would be giving people a laundry list of physical diagnoses and that that would be the bulk of the reading. As I mentioned before, I had no idea that for every physical manifestation there is an emotional, mental, or spiritual component behind it.*
Years later, after doing many readings, I can tell you with certainty that is the case *every* time. I have yet to see someone manifesting a physical

---

* Note that I have no experience with emergency cases. For example, a gunshot wound may be a different story; however, I suspect the degree to which the person recovers will tie into emotional, mental, or spiritual factors.

complaint where there was not one (or more) of the other levels acting as a component or catalyst. We break where our links are weakest. We may have fallen down a ski slope, tripped over that step, or eaten poorly and ended up weak and susceptible to another illness. That is certainly a physical "cause." Why did the fall off that stair tear the ankle ligament instead of a tendon? Why didn't the bone break? Why is there still a problem today when it happened fourteen years ago? The answer seems to be because we have not dealt with the underlying issues.

How do we know what these issues are? Let's do a little exercise. Pretend you're driving in a car. The "check engine" light comes on. What do you do? Think about this for a moment before you read further.

In workshops, my students come up with answers like these: pull over and stop; check the manual; send my car some healing; pray; call a mechanic; yell "Help!"; use my intuition to see what's wrong; call the auto club; put a yellow "sticky note" over the light so that I can't see the problem; ignore it. Generally, we take action when we think the car may be in trouble. We give it regular maintenance, tune-ups, and oil changes. When was the last time you gave yourself some regular maintenance, for example, a massage? Or perhaps that alone time you've been longing for, to read a book or just be quiet? If your car is running a little rough, one of the first things you might consider is putting in a better grade of gas. If your body is running a little less smoothly, do you consider putting in better food? Many times we do not give our bodies the same amount of sustenance, care, or timely attention that we give to our automobiles. I know many doctors who say the following scenario is not uncommon:

PATIENT: "Doctor, I have headaches."
DOCTOR: "And how long have you had these headaches?"

PATIENT: "Five years."
DOCTOR: "When did you first seek medical attention
for this condition?"
PATIENT: "Today."

It is easy to fall into thinking that if our knee hurts, we can take an aspirin. True, the pain goes away for a little while, but in reality, have we gotten to the cause of the problem? Drugs can be very helpful, if used therapeutically. But when drugs or other treatments are used to mask a problem instead of getting to the bottom of it, we can end up in worse health than before. I teach my clients and students to watch for their own personal "check engine" lights to get to the cause of a problem. Each person has more than one "check engine" light and different symptoms mean different things. For example, if your knee acts up, tune in (I'll teach how to do this in section 2) and ask your intuition what other components might be contributing to this condition (physical, mental, emotional, or spiritual). Take steps to alleviate these issues and remember them the next time your knee (the "check engine" light for this set of issues) acts up. Then, you can respond accordingly. Eventually, you can work to get these issues out of your life, and hopefully experience little or no knee problems as well. Just like a car, if you don't pay attention to your body and maintain it, you may end up with problems that are expensive or impossible to fix. Each person's "check engine" lights are different. And the physical, mental, emotional, and spiritual care that each person needs to seek will be individual.

CHAPTER 3

What Is a Reading?

When I do a reading, I tune in to my client by focusing on his or her name and age. I do not meet my clients beforehand, so I am not guessing what is wrong with them by their appearance. When I conduct the reading for the client (or the health care practitioner), he or she validates or refutes my intuitive impressions.

You can focus on anything that is connected to the person you want to read, for example, an address or a photograph. Or you could use something the person has touched, such as a piece of paper or a soft drink can (this can be very helpful in police work, when a name is unknown). When I conducted research for my master's degree, each intuitive I surveyed used at least one thing related to a client as a focal point. Sometimes my clients forget to supply me with their age, or their handwriting is so artistic that I cannot read their last name. Despite the lack of information, my intuition still works. I try not to become caught up in thinking that "it has to be a certain way" to do a reading. Being willing to work with whatever is provided keeps me flexible and unlimited.

I do the reading before my telephone session with the client. After so much practice on so many people, the health information comes to me quickly, so I type it. In the early days, when I still had grave doubts about my ability, I experienced incredible nervousness before every reading. I believed that clients were saying I was accurate to avoid hurting my feelings. To keep from receiving any clues from a client during a reading, I wrote out my intuitive impressions ahead of time. I believed this might help to prove whether (or not) my intuitive ability was real.

Some medical intuitives ask a client, "What's wrong?" first, and then explain why to the client. I initially resisted this strategy. I reasoned that by doing the reading without talking to the client first, my wild imagination (which is not the same as my intuition) would remain untantalized (the left-brain function of my imagination loves to make up stories when it knows what is wrong with a client). This method seemed to add to the credibility of the reading—clients often expressed amazement at the accuracy of the content and the fact that nothing (or very little) was overlooked.

Over time, I have developed other ways of reading people. One of them *is* to be more interactive and ask what is wrong up front. The type of reading I will do is indicated at the time I tune in. Neither the client nor I seem to control the decision over which technique is used, but the method always seems appropriate for the situation. For example, incest survivors who feel violated, people who have done a great deal of work on themselves, or people who want specific questions answered seem to benefit from a more interactive reading. Most of my readings, however, are conducted in the "lecture" format, in which I tune in ahead of time and then tell the client what I intuit, without asking first what is wrong.

WHAT'S IN A READING?

Many of the people who contact me for a reading find the information I give them validating. At the beginning of my career, I wanted to impart new and dazzling insights to each client during his or her forty-five- to sixty-minute phone appointment. I felt a little disappointed when some people said: "Thank you for being so accurate. I loved this reading! However, you haven't told me anything very different from what I've told myself, or what my best friend [doctor, pharmacist, minister, therapist, spouse] has been telling me for a long time."

Then one day a client told me: "Because you are a total stranger, with no knowledge of me other than my name and age, and who therefore has no hidden agenda with me, I finally believe this is good advice, even though I've heard it many times before from others who know and care about me. I am now motivated to change." Now I understand what's important: whether the information is old or new, dazzling or the same thing they have heard a hundred times before, what matters is whether it's accurate and beneficial to my clients.

Some clients tell me that the information I have given them is not so different from what they've been told by their doctor, minister, best friend, spouse, and even themselves. However, as my client pointed out above, because I am a complete stranger, know only their name and age, have no hidden agenda, and have a record of being very accurate, they are more willing to accept the information I give them. If that's what it takes to motivate and transform them, I'm all for it.

Additionally, I receive information on modes of treatment and avenues of change that a client may choose to pursue. I try to offer choices of ways they can improve their health and well-being. Choices are important; mandates are disempowering. I never want to be the kind of intuitive who encourages her clients to rely on her only, rather than on themselves. As one of my clients said, "Thanks for the road map. I'll take it from here."

I do not use formulas to evaluate clients. I thought that after a hundred readings or so, most people would fall into a few categories, and I could just reel off their readings without working too hard. I was wrong. Everyone is different. Each reading is customized. And although I do see certain overall patterns, there are always exceptions.

When analyzing yourself, you can use the information contained in section 1 to give you clues that may determine the cause of your problems, but there is one way to be sure of their source: by learning to use your own intuition (as taught in section 2). This is why I suggest you learn to tune in yourself. Don't memorize and rely *only* on previously learned information; let your intuition flow. You'll be surprised at the new impressions or insights that come through.

Every reading is different, yet after doing readings for a short while, I began to notice patterns that were common to many people, including me. These patterns can be found on any level: physical, mental, emotional, or spiritual. In the following pages, I'll go over ways to overcome patterns of thinking and behavior that can have a destructive effect on your life and your health. If what you read resonates and keeps coming to your attention, that's a big clue that your intuition is speaking to you. And who knows what's best for you better than that little voice inside your head?

CHAPTER 4

What's My Problem? What's My Priority?

In the following chapters, I will go through concerns that my clients, students, and many other people face. These issues include building the right foundation for health; overcoming the habit mind; learning nonphysical ways to increase energy; dealing with people and situations that drain energy; regaining balance in life; and transcending emotional issues such as worry, guilt, fear, control, judgment, anger, and depression. To determine which concerns are important to you, pay attention to how you feel as you are reading along.

We can't simultaneously work on every issue that is facing us. We have to set priorities, or we will become overwhelmed. Through working with clients and students, I have found there are generally three kinds of responses that people have to issues. I call these responses *key indicators*, and they are your clues to which issues are priorities for you. One key indicator involves feelings of anger, irritation, or frustration. This type of response indicates a priority issue for you. For example, you may be reading about a certain type of physical exercise, and the more you read, the angrier you become. *There's nothing new here! I've wasted my money on this book!* you might think.

In reading about another issue, however, you may feel nonchalant or neutral: *I know this, but it's still interesting.* This second type of response usually indicates that this area is not a place of concern for you. You probably do not have a major issue with the topic at hand, or you have worked through it already.

On the other hand, you may feel sleepy when you read about a certain issue and have to keep refocusing your eyes, rereading what you have just read, or you may find you cannot remember the words you just read. This is the third type of key indicator. These are the big issues, the ones you may not be ready for yet.

I would suggest working on the "irritable" issues first, then the "sleepy/I-can't-remember" issues. If you want to keep track of your priorities, use a small notebook or write in this book. Note the date, too, because next year, or the next time you pick up this book, it will be interesting to see how you have changed.

I've listed only a few of the reactions you might encounter. Pay attention to any shifts you feel as you are reading along. For example, one of my Canadian students told me that during one of my lectures, her vision blurred every time I talked about what she considered a prime issue for her. In Stamford, Connecticut, an audience member said that he felt his body temperature go up each time one of his "hot button" problem areas was discussed. Learn to listen to your own signals to know what you need to focus on. As you work on your issues, you may find you need help from another person. If you need some support, avail yourself of a friend, spiritual resource, or counselor.

CHAPTER 5

Building the Right Foundation

Overall, I have been most surprised by my intuitive findings in the area of nutrition. From the beginning, I've encountered an amazing number of malnourished people. *Webster's New World Dictionary* defines *malnutrition* as "poor nourishment resulting from insufficient food, improper diet, etc." The bulk of my clients are Americans. At first, I could not fathom how the nutrition of citizens of the richest country in the world could be so poor. Even though I did not have in-person contact with my clients, from looking at most Americans, I would not have guessed that they are malnourished—they do not look overly thin, like a person experiencing famine would, for example. Malnourishment in America was a huge intuitive revelation to me. I now believe that, for the majority of Americans, it has two main causes: a poor choice of food and inconsistent eating habits.

As I do a reading, I ask my intuition many questions. Fascinated by what I was seeing in the area of diet, I asked why nutrition is so important. The answer I found can be summed up like this: Imagine a house with a poor foundation or no foundation at all. How can it support itself, weather the elements, and stay strong in a storm? Your body is like that house. Without a good nutritional foundation, how can you hope to have good health? Sooner or later, poor nutrition catches up with you.

I used to ask clients, "How's your nutrition?"

"Oh, pretty good. I eat healthy foods," they might respond.

I'd tune in and say, "What are these Hostess bakery products I see you with? You know, like Ding Dongs."

"Oh. Well, I like their Ho Hos and Cup Cakes. But I only eat them on the way to work." (This client worked six days a week—that's a lot of Cup Cakes.)

Or I would say, "It seems that you eat quite a few sweets."

"No."

"What's this yellow sponge cake I'm seeing?"

"Oh. That. Well, only one slice a day, after lunch and after dinner, that is."

Now that I'm more experienced, I ask the right question: "What do you eat?" The responses are more revealing. Most people are not educated in nutrition. A friend of mine in the health field told me that doctors receive only one hour of nutrition education in medical school. Everyone, from laypeople to physicians, can benefit from improved nutritional education. Based on what I have intuitively seen, I would say that 70 percent of Americans are malnourished. I've spoken to other holistic health care practitioners and physicians, and most estimate 60 to 80 percent. Lack of proper nutrition is a serious problem.

CASE STUDIES

To give you an idea of how widespread malnourishment is—and the different ways in which poor nutrition manifests itself—here are a couple of case studies.

As I tuned in to Albert, I kept getting impressions of him working out, driving a lot, and eating "unreal" food. I did not understand
this impression until we spoke. Albert explained that he was a personal trainer who spent a lot of time keeping himself looking good
and driving from one appointment to the next to coach clients. As a
result, he was too busy to prepare and eat good meals. Instead, he
subsisted mostly on replacement meals (shakes, powders mixed with
liquid, etc.). He was eating almost no "real" food and definitely no
whole foods. As a result, his body was experiencing some interesting
breakdowns throughout various organs and his immune and muscu-
loskeletal systems. From the outside, he looked great; on the inside,
he had no building blocks to sustain his health. He was run-down
and heading for a health crash.

Another client, Margarete, seemed to be poisoning herself with
vitamins. I did not understand how this was possible until I spoke
with Margarete and her physician. In doing Margarete's reading, I
kept feeling like her bones were being poisoned. I felt confused when
I tried to discern the cause, as it felt like supplements and some type
of tribal (club) activity were responsible for this problem, so I asked
Margarete. She explained that she belonged to a multilevel marketing company (MLM) that sold vitamins, minerals, and other supplements. An MLM is a business practice that is similar to a club in
which the members who belong buy products and ask people they
know to join and buy as well. At meetings, members are strongly
encouraged to buy and try all of the products. There is a sort of competition among them to see who is taking the most of each supplement. This became extreme for Margarete. For example, she was
putting vitamins in her drinking water. Her doctor confirmed my
intuitive finding regarding the damage to her bones and its physical
cause (overtaking supplements). My client was devastated.
Margarete felt she had no life and no friends outside of her MLM.
She believed that if she practiced moderation, she might save her

health, but she would certainly be alone. We worked on her emotional issues, and she decided to seek further assistance through her physician and psychotherapist.

In the current "no-fat/low-fat" processed food environment, I am seeing more and more people whose bodies are manifesting dryness, in the skin or elsewhere, because they are not getting the right kinds of oils and fats in their diets. We do need *good* oils and fats in our diets. One way to find out which components are missing in your diet is to consult with a nutritionist to determine what the right kinds of fats and oils are for you and whether you need supplements or can get these from foods.

Plenty of fruits and vegetables, fresh and preferably organic, go a long way toward energizing our systems. I see many vegetarians, however, with poor nutrition and sometimes a protein deficiency. A vegetarian can eat just as much junk as a meat-eater can. If you do not eat meat but include doughnuts or french fries as a consistent part of your daily food program, you're playing nutritional Russian roulette.

Nutrition is an individual thing. There is no one right plan that works for everyone or even for a majority of people. For example, some people need to have meat in their diets; others do better without it. When determining the best diet for yourself, make sure that it is balanced and full of nutritionally rich foods, not junk.

Junk food comes in many disguises. Sam, a wonderful client, was diagnosed with pancreatic cancer. He told me, "I'll do anything to save my pancreas."

I said, "How about a bigger perspective: 'I'll do anything to change my life'?" He agreed that he was highly invested in saving his cancerous pancreas, but if it were not possible, the larger perspective could do more good and could keep devastating disappointment at bay. We talked about nutrition. He said he thoroughly understood what I was trying to tell him. "But it's still okay to eat Cauldron

Chips, right? I won't have to give them up, will I?" he asked.

"Cauldron Chips," sold almost exclusively by health-food stores, are touted as a more healthful version of potato chips, made with better oil and containing fewer additives. I've looked at their label. They are a highly processed food. Sam would do anything to save his pancreas, but he wouldn't give up his food habit. We decided that a nutritionist and some form of counseling to deal with his detrimental thought patterns and emotional ties to food would be good avenues of support.

MALABSORPTION

Another area of malnutrition is malabsorption. I've seen that many of my clients cannot absorb the nutrition in the food—healthy or not—that they are ingesting. I believe that inconsistency of diet is the most important cause of malabsorption.

My theory is that some people who eat only one healthy meal per day—for example, dinner—consider their diet healthy. Their breakfast is a bagel, their lunch is fast food, and their dinner is stir-fried vegetables. It's my theory that their poor bodies don't know which kind of food is coming down the pike. The result? I think that the body does not absorb as much of the food because it is never sure of the nutritional value or damage that is contained in that food. Although this is only my personal theory, I have talked to other health care practitioners who have arrived at similar conclusions.

One of my clients had the worst colon health I had ever seen in a reading. After I diplomatically brought this to his attention, Ed admitted that his bowel movements lasted up to six hours at a time. As a result, he could not work, had been on welfare for six years, and was in danger of becoming homeless. I said, "It seems to me you have been eating lots of greasy fast food when you would be better served by raw whole foods."

"I did that!" he exclaimed. "I went to a clinic in southern California and ate raw whole foods for six weeks. It *almost* cured me."

"Why haven't you continued?" I asked.

"*Almost!*" he replied. "It didn't completely cure me, so I didn't stick with it."

Ed is fifty-three years old. It takes more than six weeks to correct a lifetime of poor nutritional habits. I call this type of healing "MTV healing," after the fast-paced video network that is famous for its three-second visual clips. Certainly, miracles can happen. You can even expect them. But, for most people, myself included, it takes time to adjust. Caroline Myss, Ph.D., a medical intuitive and author, says, "You expect instant healing, but you aren't ready for instant change." Does this apply to you?

WHAT TO DO

If your eating habits are even the least bit questionable or you feel your health is at risk because of poor nutrition, you need to be proactive about changing your diet. What should you do? Oftentimes, in my readings, I suggest to my clients that they consult an open-minded, holistic, certified nutritionist for counseling and education. You, too, could consider doing this. Such a nutritionist isn't going to give you a one-size-fits-all program, but instead will listen to you and apply all of his or her experience (and possibly some intuition!) to create a customized diet that works for you. Sometimes spending money to get that one-on-one attention saves time and expense in the long run. Think about it this way: Nutritionists have spent years learning about nutrition; they are experts in the field. You could do the research yourself, but even if you read ten books, you might not know nearly as much as they know. It may take a long time to read those ten books—and what if they are not the right resources for you? Learn what works for you, specifically, and how to change your habits. If you visited a nutritionist twenty years ago, your needs may have changed, so another session may be of benefit.

If working one-on-one with a nutritionist is not feasible, take a class in which you can learn from a good teacher and interested students. If a consultation or class is not affordable right now, check out books, magazine articles, and other resources from your local library. Stay away from complicated or fad diets—go for solid and proven nutritional principles. Moderation and consistency are key.

BASIC NUTRITIONAL TERMS AND DEFINITIONS

I have found that even the basic principles of nutrition and its definitions elude most of my clients and students. I am not saying you should eat only certain foods; however, if you eat a balanced diet, you will experience better nutrition, which can lead to better health. The following are some basic terms, but for the whole picture and your own needs, please consult a professional resource.

Processed Foods

Processed foods have been processed in a manufacturing plant or a factory. Food in a can, for example, has been processed. In the case of pasta, wheat has been made into flour, then bleached, fortified, and artificially colored before it becomes spaghetti. This is processed. You want to aim for foods that have as little processing and as few artificial flavors and colors as possible. Annemarie Colbin, in her excellent nutritional reference, *Food and Healing*, explains why. She states that plants and animals are living systems. The original qualities of these systems are passed on when they are used as food. The more time that elapses from the moment they are harvested, and the more changes that take place through processing, the less nourishment they will offer.[1]

Whole Foods

Whole foods include cooked or raw foods that are not missing any edible parts, such as a whole apple, complete with the skin. Whole grains are grains that have not lost any of their edible parts through processing. Why should we strive for whole instead of fragmented foods? Think of it this way: Until recently, humans had been eating foods in a more whole, less processed form. Colbin uses the example of eating whole wheat instead of consuming wheat germ, white flour, and bran separately. When we eat foods that are not whole—say, white bread—we might be missing the wheat germ and the bran. For thousands of years, humans have evolved to eat all the parts of foods together, not just some of them or separately. If we are not designed to properly digest nonwhole foods, we are not able to derive full nutrition from them. Therefore, we should try to eat as many whole foods (i.e., whole fruits and vegetables, unrefined grains, beans, nuts, etc.) as possible, as this is what our bodies are intended to use. Colbin sums up this concept nicely: "Whole foods provide not only certain amounts of basic nutrients in the natural proportion to each other; the nutrients in them are also bound together by that subtle energy that animates all living systems. Whole foods, then, give us not only nutrition, but energy—'wholesomeness' that is."[2]

Raw Foods

Raw foods are as close to their natural (uncooked) state as possible. Humans have not always cooked and processed everything, so again, we are not as evolved for "un-raw" foods. Additionally, foods are usually the most nutritious in the raw state. As nutritionist Kymthy Schultze states: "Cooking actually changes the molecular structure of food. Cooking or heat processing binds food molecules tighter together, making them more difficult to digest and transforms them into 'foreign' or unfamiliar food. Cooked food takes longer to digest and therefore requires more energy. Heat also destroys enzymes and anitoxidants . . . [which] impairs the immune system."[3] Some of my client's digestive systems are so sensitive (see chapter 8 for more information on sensitivity) that they cannot handle raw foods. Also, if someone has been eating a highly processed diet, he or she will need to transition to food in its more natural state. Lightly steamed or cooked foods are gentler on the system and still retain more nutrition than something that is cooked until it is nearly unrecognizable.

Supplements

Our soil is depleted. This contributes to a lower nutrient composition in food. Most health care practitioners agree that vitamins and minerals can help supplement what you cannot get in food. Remember, a *supplement* is not a *replacement*. Many of my clients think they can eat fast food every day, and as long as they take their vitamins, they will be fine. This has not been my experience. Additionally, overdoing vitamins can have a poisoning or unbalancing effect on your body (as shown in Margarete's reading). Check with your health care practitioner to find out if you need supplements and, if so, what the right combination is for you.

Consistency is key. Be creative. Make it convenient to eat well by having lots of healthy food around you. Take baby steps as you transition. Instead of that yellow sponge cake at lunch and dinner, substitute an apple. Small steps seem to work well. If you hate to cook, consider hiring someone to cook for you. A friend of mine hires college kids to cook for her for minimum wage. She provides the food and recipes, and three hours later, the students have prepared a whole week's worth of healthy food. If your family is unsupportive of your change, don't be discouraged. Your life is worth the investment in spite of a lack of support. You can eat in a healthy way and let them be responsible for what they consume. Many times, loved ones come around as they see the vital and healthful changes you experience. You can serve as an example to them.

Most important, don't expect to change overnight. Certainly, eating "clean" food can result in better energy and health improvements, but a lifetime of poor food habits that have affected your health may take time to overcome.

According to the information in the readings I have conducted, these are some of the food concepts and habits you may want to incorporate into your diet. Remember, take the self-test to gain insight into the importance of this issue for you. Were you irritated, annoyed, or angry as you read this chapter on nutrition? If so, examine this area more closely. Based on my work, these types of feelings usually mean this is a priority issue. If you were feeling sleepy or cannot remember what you just read, chances are this is an even bigger issue for you—you might want to work through other priorities before addressing this one. If you felt a neutral interest while reading this chapter, you may not need to focus a great deal on this area. What if you were simply very interested, even enthusiastic? Often, my intuition communicates to me through what appeals. I'll hear about something new, and all of a sudden, my breath quickens a little, a smile plays on my lips, and I start to get excited. I let my interest lead me to a newfound passion. If you find this is the case with you, let your feelings guide you to new knowledge.

I am not a nutritionist, so I cannot give you complete information about what type of diet is best for you, but support is available. As I have discovered information intuitively (nutritional or otherwise), it seems that resources come along to confirm my findings. Most of what I have encountered is validated in Annemarie Colbin's book, *Food and Healing*.[4] She provides much more detail, specifics, and research. I have found her book to be the most congruent with the information provided to me intuitively. As with any change you make in your health program, it is important to check with your health care practitioner first, to make sure the change is in your best interest. You are worth the investment of a good nutritional program.

CHAPTER 6

The Habit Mind

There are important differences in the definitions of *habit* and *addiction*. Addiction experts define *habit* as something you can stop at will, whereas *addiction* is a multifaceted medical term that can encompass chemical dependency, mental health issues, and genetic factors. *Webster's New World Dictionary* defines *habit* as "a pattern of action that is acquired and has become so automatic that it is difficult to break." The word *addiction* doesn't usually come through when I do a reading. Instead, I get the word *habit*. Why? Intuitively, I have been told that *addiction* is a charged word, a hot button in our culture. Being called an addict can have a stigma attached to it. *Habit* is a more acceptable term to many people. I need people to be able to hear me when I am speaking to them. If I use a word that causes them to "turn off" when they hear it, it is of no use. I go with the wording that gets the message across. It's not a matter of deception; I am simply trying to get the communication through in whatever way it can be received. Once my clients hear the message, they can use it to access the help they need.

Throughout this chapter and this book, I will use the word *habit* as that is the common term I get when I read for people and the term I am most comfortable conveying. In no way am I trying to demean someone suffering from addiction. Intuitively, I see addiction as having the aspect of a habit, but much more intensified, and therefore, very difficult to break on one's own. Although this chapter speaks to the habit mind, I believe the principles are sound and can be used to help someone suffering from full-fledged addiction.

HEART-MIND INCONGRUENCE

Caroline Myss taught me that addictions and detrimental habits reside in the will chakra (the throat energy center). They come about when the mind and the heart are incongruent. This incongruence can lead to a "lack of dialogue" between heart and mind. Since the will center is located physically in between these two areas, it suffers, and addiction and detrimental habits happen.

Look at yourself. What incongruencies are occurring between your heart and mind? Do you hate your job (heart) but need the money to make the mortgage (mind)? Do you want to leave your partner (heart) but feel trapped as if you have no choice (mind)? Do you do things that compromise your integrity (mind) but feel afraid to stand up for what you believe (heart)? These are just a few examples of tough questions many people face. To answer them, my clients and students try to find compromises that work toward a future of greater heart-mind congruency. This thought pattern is found the world over. The Indian sage Paramahansa Yogananda said, "Unite the heart's feeling and the mind's reason in a perfect balance."[1]

TYPES OF HABITS

What habits (and addictions) do I most commonly see in clients? If you think drugs, alcohol, smoking, and sex are at the top of the list, you are wrong. Food, shopping, worry, guilt, blame/victimization, self-criticism, emotionally or physically rescuing and fixing others' lives, negative attitudes, blaming, television, and spirituality (religion or New Age—it doesn't matter) are just a few of the common ones.

Some habits, when practiced in moderation and with consistency, are healthy, but anything that affects our lives and thoughts negatively can be a problem. One way to work on unhealthy habits is to replace them with healthy ones. Unhealthy habits can affect you on all levels—physically, emotionally, mentally, and spiritually—but by addressing heart-mind incongruencies, you can begin to transcend these behaviors and work toward improved health and well-being.

HOW TO CHANGE

How do you transcend incongruencies between heart and mind and thus help the habit mind? Through dialogue and negotiation. Talk to your heart and your mind. It might sound silly, but it works (and it's free!). Ask your heart what it wants. Wait for the answer. Do the same for your mind. Work out a deal between the two. Such a dialogue might go like this: "Okay heart, how about if we take that painting class I've been promising myself for years? We'll start *now*. And mind, let's figure out a plan where I can save enough money at this job to take a sabbatical or a cut in pay to do something I really love." This is different from bargaining with something unhealthy, for example, spending your free time gambling instead of drinking alcohol in bars. How do you know the difference between unhealthy bargaining and healthy negotiation? If you have trouble telling, then get help and support from a trained professional or a recovery organization.

Healthy dialogue and action can and do work for the habit mind. How many times have you lied to yourself? "I'll start this exercise program January 1," you might resolve. When you don't start exercising, you rationalize, "Well, I didn't say *this* January." Or you might promise to eat better, but you never do. Lying to yourself is a form of incongruency that can easily lead to other unhealthy habits. Be aware of how many promises you make to yourself. Do you keep them? If you can't, don't make them. Or, perhaps, make smaller ones. Start with small steps and work up to the big changes.

CASE STUDIES

One of my best friends found himself depressed, moody, and lacking motivation to do much more than go to work, sit on the couch, and watch TV. Juan knew he needed a substitute for these unhealthy tendencies. He considered what he wanted to do instead, and checked in with his heart and mind. Juan has replaced these behaviors, which he found undesirable and unhealthy, with a mountain biking habit. He is not overzealous. Juan bikes perhaps one evening a week in the summer and year-round on weekends. To him, it is more than exercise or something that has lifted him out of his moodiness and mild depression. Biking offers him solitude, concentration, and time in nature—his form of spiritual practice. For him, spirituality does not have to encompass a specific religion; he knows how to connect to spirit any time—it is within him.

Gina positively craves yoga once a week. She uses this to replace her soap opera habit. You may laugh at Gina's habit and think it is inconsequential, but remember that anything that influences our lives and thoughts negatively can be a problem. She noticed that thinking throughout the day about the pessimistic plot lines of soap operas was making her feel more negative about her life. She was missing a creative outlet for her body and a way to calm her mind. Gina found that practicing yoga had a much more positive impact on her than watching imaginary people create problems. Her heart is happy: it has found a creative outlet for the body. Her mind is happy: it has found a break that is calming instead of negative. Whatever you use as a substitute (e.g., yoga, mountain biking, reading, creative expression), remember that moderation and consistency are key.

Until I read for Josh, I had never gotten the term *alcoholic* in a reading. In Josh's case, such a serious problem needed to be directly addressed. He was ready for such a direct hit. When I asked him, "Do you think you're an alcoholic?" he replied, "I have been seriously considering it. Now that it has come up in this reading, I'm ready to do something about it." Josh decided to seek professional treatment; however, aspects of the habit mind came into play as causes for his problem. Josh is a wonderful musician and interested in theatrical arts, but he was not pursuing this passion. Instead, he worked as a bartender in a nightclub, where he was tantalized by seeing others living their dreams of musicianship. Night after night, he was reminded that he wasn't pursuing his love. His heart wanted music; his mind said, "We need this high-paying job because we have an expensive mortgage, and we like all of the things that a lot of money can buy." His heart and mind were incongruent, and his will was left out of the picture. Working in a nightclub, as a bartender, the wrong solution was all around him: alcohol. He began to drink. Eventually, he drank all of the time and couldn't stop. To give his heart something it needed, Josh decided after his reading with me to volunteer in a community theater program. Additionally, he developed a plan to quit his job. He also decided to get professional help. He is now recovering and plans to pursue his musical dreams with the awareness and tools he needs to avoid getting into a future habit or addiction that will not bring him happiness and health.

Just as you did with the nutrition chapter, take the self-test to gain insight into the importance of the habit-mind issue for you. Were you irritated, annoyed, or angry, as you read this chapter? If so, examine this area more closely—this could be a priority for you. If you were feeling sleepy or cannot remember what you just read, chances are this is an even bigger issue for you. You might want to put it on the back burner, to look at after you've worked through other priorities. If you felt a neutral kind of interest while reading this chapter, you may not need to focus a great deal on this area.

Through my work as an intuitive, these are the steps that I have found to be effective for clients and students who want to transcend their unhealthy habits: healthy substitution, negotiation, dialogue, and being truthful with yourself. If a habit is too overwhelming to change by yourself, work in partnership with others. Get the support you need, be it a friend, a support group, or a professional counselor. Become aware, talk to your heart and mind, don't lie to yourself, take baby steps, and substitute more healthful habits for the detrimental ones. Such steps are simple, albeit challenging, and just like anything else, change takes intention and practice, practice, practice.

CHAPTER 7

Nonphysical Ways to Increase Your Energy

It seems like one of the most common problems my clients and students have is lack of energy. This can manifest itself in many ways, from a complete lack of vitality (for example, a client is bedridden or unable to work because he or she is so tired) to a block of expression and motivation (a client just can't drag himself or herself to work at that job, relationship, exercise program, etc., anymore). Be it fatigue or an inability to summon up power on any level to live the life they want to live, lack of energy is a potent block that frustrates many people.

The two best ways I know to increase energy are through *release* and *divine connection*. Working with these two areas can increase your life energy, health, and well-being. Divine connection gives energy; release frees up energy that is caught in the past.

DIVINE CONNECTION

Why do I use the term *divine connection*? Many people have an aversion to the word *prayer*. I can empathize. After leaving the Catholic religion behind, I positively cringed at the word for fifteen years. I have no problem with it now, but I have learned through my teaching and client consultations that if someone is uncomfortable with a word, they may shut down and be unable to hear or read further. That is why I have chosen the more benign term *divine connection*. If you prefer a different word, substitute *affirmation, prayer, statement, energy, spirit, intention,* or whatever you like.

The word *intention* comes through often in my readings. What is an intention? It is the desire, or determination, to act or be a certain way. It is a statement of what you are directing your energy toward. I find the word *intention* an excellent substitute for the term *prayer* because both words are defined as "directing energy and attention."

Although my clients can choose to connect divinely in a religious setting or a sacred shrine, I also suggest the option of being less formal. Connection can happen any time, any place. I love the title of the book *Conversations with God*[1] because I think it brings to people's attention the idea that prayer can be friendly and conversational—a back-and-forth dialogue.

Whom do you dialogue with? Each person's preference is perfect for him or her. Some people feel it is a source outside of themselves, some feel it is within them, and some feel it is a mixture of both. I advise clients and students not to get caught up in labels—*God, Buddha, Jesus, Allah, Brahma, etc.*—if these designations get in the way of the connection. Some people are comfortable with these terms, while some may prefer others, such as *inner guidance, higher self, the universe, higher power, energy, goddess, nature, spirit*—you name it, I've heard it. The label doesn't matter; the divine connection does. You may find that your connection has changed over the years. One of my clients was taught to use the name *Father* or *Jesus* as a child. As she grew into young womanhood, she was drawn to the term *goddess* but felt as though she was being sacrilegious by abandoning the words taught to her as a young girl. She worked through the underlying issue—that of creating a divine relationship on her own terms—and as she shifted and changed, her divine label did too. The profeminist twenty-year-old metamorphosed into a calmer, gentler woman in her forties. Her choice of labels reflects her shift. She now uses the word *spirit* to denote her divine connection.

46

Having a different relationship with the divine as a child, teenager, and adult is perfectly fine. Many people feel it is disrespectful to change. They stay with the religion or ideas they were born into, even if they no longer work for them. One of my clients called herself a "cult-hopper." For more than twenty years, she went from organized religion to New-Age fad to cult, trying to find herself and her personal connection. At the end of this cycle, she found it hard to pray or to have any sort of divine connection that did not remind her of her past, which she wanted to leave behind. Together, we came up with a creative way around the problem. She decided to write a letter to the divine. She didn't have to "speak" or "think" her connection in her head, reminding her of her past search for organized spirituality; she could do something different. She decided to set up a new kind of relationship, and writing a letter seemed like the perfect creative way to begin.

Having relationships that work for you, at this time in your life, is of great importance. As we change, our relationships do too. Are you still friends with everyone you knew twenty years ago? Probably not. Even if you have long-standing relationships, are they the same every year, or even every month? Again, probably not. Why should your divine connection remain the same? It can change as you change.

It is important to be honest in your relationship with the divine. Just as you would tell a dear friend if you were upset about something, instead of holding on to resentment that would affect the friendship, you need to communicate to the divine when you are unhappy. Don't let regret, anger, or resentment get in the way of a fulfilling relationship. Get it off your chest. The old fear that you will be punished if you are angry with God is continually disproved in my intuitive readings. If you want a complete, honest, and fulfilling relationship with anyone, including the divine, keep it clean. Say what's on your mind, no matter what it is. Anger at the divine is the most common roadblock I see to spiritual connection, and it can lead to health concerns as well. Communicate everything, in whatever way works for you.

There are many ways to connect, but I have found that conversation is a comfortable format for many people. Remember, the connection is a conversation, not a monologue. Make it a give-and-take dialogue. Listen, instead of just talking or asking. This happens within you. No one needs to know that you are connecting—it can be completely private. A simple thing, like saying, "Thank you for this beautiful day," is a wonderful form of divine connection. Perhaps you'll start to hear a soft, "You're welcome." Cultivating this relationship may take a bit of time, like building a new friendship or learning to play the piano. As you grow in confidence, clear, accurate guidance begins coming through. And what more is intuition than divine guidance? It's divine because it's through you, a divine being.

With time, you may shift to a place where the connection is so much a part of you that you instinctively know the right way to live your life and how to make decisions. Some cultures call this "right living." You feel congruent with the divine self, and therefore act and serve by example. Serving by example, living your life in a way that is absolutely interconnected with your spirit, is a beautiful form of divine connection. Being of service to others is a great gift to humanity.

My spiritual mentor, George, works for a small company. He could probably work elsewhere, for more money, but that's not what it's about for him. While completing his regular job duties, he spends his day as the unofficial human resource person (he has another job title), helping co-workers through their life crises and spiritual dilemmas. He never lectures them or tries to control them, but instead offers wisdom, resources, and a listening ear. He lives his life in a simple way, full of kindness. He exemplifies his divine connection by living a life that is congruent with his spirit. It inspires and guides others to have the courage to do the same.

Guidance is not the only reason to cultivate divine connection.

Another important benefit is that it can increase energy. I have seen this happen many times.

Years ago, I was privileged to take a workshop with visionary artist Alex Grey. Alex's depiction of the human energy system in *Sacred Mirrors* is one of the most beautiful things I have ever seen.[2] During the workshop, Alex instructed us to view the individual chakras (the seven major energy centers in the body) of a live model and draw what we saw. As the only nonartist in the group (I brought my crayons), I had to rely on my inner sight instead of my undeveloped art talent to participate in the exercise. I tuned in to our live model. As I intuitively "looked" at each of her energy centers, I noticed that for a woman who was young (twenty-four) and healthy by outward appearance, her chakras were strangely out of sync with each other. Additionally, their colors were neither bright nor clearly delineated, as one would expect in a healthy energy system.

When the session progressed to the sixth chakra—traditionally the seat of the mind, wisdom, and intuition—Alex put on meditative music and placed the model in a sitting meditation pose. Immediately, her chakras began to turn in rhythm with each other (*chakra* is Sanskrit for *wheel*). Their colors cleaned up, taking on individual hues appropriate to their fields.

For the seventh chakra, the traditional repository of divine connection and grace, Alex played music inspired by spiritual traditions and folded our model's hands together while she looked upward, in a contemplative, prayerlike pose. I saw a silvery energy pouring in through the top of her head and into each and every chakra, feeding her energy.

After the session was over, I spoke to the model. Not wanting to ask her a leading question about what I had seen, I asked what she did while holding long poses. She said, "I was so glad to be put in the meditative pose, because I haven't meditated in days—it felt so good to do it. During the prayer pose, I prayed."

From this experience, I realized that meditation aligns the energies of the body, and divine connection feeds them. An aligned energy system indicates balance and works efficiently, with the least amount of drain on the system. Think of it like a car that has been tuned up: the spark plugs fire at precisely the right time, and the efficiency of the engine is maximized. Consider the divine connection as an unlimited supply of the cleanest, most appropriate "fuel" possible for the system. In the case of a car, with regular maintenance, it will run smoothly, without breaking down.

Although you may think, *What do I have in common with a machine?* any scientist or medical professional will tell you that our bodies are electromagnetic systems. They are energy in physical and nonphysical forms. The growing field of energy medicine (in which I hold a master's degree) works with and tests these energies.

Again, clients validate these findings. I can tell when someone has an active divine connection—what some call a "prayer life"—when I look at them intuitively. No matter how sick a person may be, this connection provides him or her with benefits. For example, a client may be ill, but I will notice an absence of the most common major fear I see: the fear of being alone. This is the number-one fear I see in people. It comes in many guises—fears of being homeless, dying alone, being alone in old age, not having a significant other, being neglected by children and friends, being alone because of illness— the manifestations are endless. Once one feels a divine connection, one is never alone. And once one can be alone with the divine self, other relationships come easily, richly, better than ever. I have seen this happen more times than I can count. The fear of being alone can be dissipated by pursuing a relationship with the divine, in whatever form you find it. Cultivate your divine link—it is one of the best ways to increase your life energy, health, and well-being.

RELEASE

There is one other potent way to increase energy through nonphysical means: release, also known as forgiveness. As with nearly everything in my work, this concept came as a surprise to me. It comes as a surprise to many of my clients and students too. Such a simple thing, but so challenging. Many people feel an aversion to the word *forgiveness*, because they think of it as a synonym for *approval*. Some people simply have a negative association with the word. To overcome these objections, I use the term *forgiveness-release* when I talk about the process.

Many authors, teachers, and speakers encourage us to release, forgive, cut the cords, or pull the plug on the past. It sounds so good. If a person can put it into practice, he or she becomes more present, instead of being caught up in the past, and thus can be clearer in the moment. This clarity leads to better decisions, increased energy, and, often, improved health and well-being.

These are powerful motivators toward forgiveness-release. However, I have found that when my clients and students try to put forgiveness or release into practice, they do not have a practical method to do so. I intuitively asked for and received a quick, three-step process. I have tested this on hundreds of students and clients, and it seems to work for the great majority of them. This simple method puts into practice the theory of forgiveness-release.

How do you know when you need to release? When you are haunted by what I call the audio- and videotapes that play in your mind. For example, have you ever been driving in your car, and, upon arriving at your destination, you realize your mind has been elsewhere the whole time? All of a sudden, you were swept up in an old memory. That is the clue that something is keeping a part of your attention or energy in the past. This is different from consciously choosing to recall a memory—that's not the problem. The difference here is that the past takes you back without your conscious permission; you haven't decided to go there. To become more present, you need to release. Getting your energy back from the past (each memory holds a little bit of your attention and energy) and into the present is a great way to heal and fully enjoy a life that flows.

The next time you catch yourself lost in the past, snapping yourself out of the reverie of a memory—whether that memory is five minutes or twenty years old—take the time to release or forgive the person, situation, or even yourself using the following steps. Each step below is only one sentence long, followed by an explanation. It takes about thirty seconds to go through this process, and the payoff can be enormous.

Step 1: *This happened in the past.* Even if something happened one minute ago, it is in the past. (Notice that you are *not* saying, "I approve of what happened"; rather, you are *acknowledging* that it happened in the past.)

Step 2: *I learned from it.* Many times, we are aware of the lesson or lessons that come from an experience. Other times, it seems that we will never know what particular lesson we are meant to receive. Trying to figure out the what, how, or why of a lesson can become an obsession. It is an exceptionally human quality to want to have answers. Sometimes we spend weeks, months, or years trying to figure out the answers. Certainly, a time of reflection to learn from an experience is important, but when the process becomes so lengthy that it drains our energy and doesn't shed new light on the matter, it is time to release. To satisfy this very human part of yourself when you cannot figure out the answers (or lessons), say, "Well, it made me the person I am today."

Step 3: *I am ready to let go, release, forgive, move on.* Use whatever words work for you—don't get caught up in my terminology.

Many times, this simple process works for my clients. Sometimes, especially with extremely painful issues, we need a boost. That's when I suggest including a fourth step: divine connection.

Optional step 4: *Divine energy* (or whatever word you want to use), *I realize that this happened in the past, I learned from it, and I am ready to let go and forgive. Help!* Again, you can use the words that work best for you. I like using *help* without any modifiers. When we put restrictions and qualifiers with our requests, we are limiting the amount of divine response we might receive. A "blank-check help" is unlimited; it can get you the fastest, best assistance available. When you put limitations on your requests, it seems to me that divine energy has to work around your parameters. A plain cry for help can end up giving you a solution you may never have thought of, but one that is more perfect than you could have imagined.

Once this process has started, it may feel like you've opened Pandora's box. Memories that you have not accessed for years begin to flood your mind. It may feel like every twenty seconds, another thing bubbles up that you need to release. Rest assured that this is a short-term condition, usually lasting from a few hours to a few days. After a time, the memory flood lessens, and you begin to feel lighter, more energized, and more present in the now, instead of distracted by the past.

Once in a while, I'll have a client who needs to reinforce this process with a physical ritual. For example, Cara decided that to help her release her toughest issue, she would write it down first. Many people find that mind mapping (a process of using a large sheet of paper, putting the main issue in the center, and connecting every association that comes to mind) is helpful in releasing the whole issue. Cara took her time and filled the page with everything she could think of that related to her issue. After going through the four forgiveness-release steps, Cara brought closure to the process. It took her a long time to find the right ritual. Rushing herself was not helpful, so finding the right time was equally important. She burned the paper and collected the ashes. She had a vision of needing to do this near a body of water. She released a small portion of the ashes, so as not to pollute. After doing this, she felt no immediate difference. Several days later, though, she noticed a calmer and more present mind, less resentment, and greater energy.

Cara's example also shows us how important it is to find the right time for forgiveness. Many people advocate instant release and a very short grieving process. They admonish, "Get on with your life!" no matter how serious the wound. I have found that if the time is not right, with forgiveness or any other issue, it does not matter what one does, it will not work. What can you do if you have something you have been working on and want to release, but you simply cannot move forward? Sometimes checking in with a friend or counselor can uncover hidden blocks. It is hard to be objective with ourselves— another perspective often can shed light. Or you can check in with your intuition (see section 2) and see if there is some additional information you need to know. Then simply and gently hold the intention that you will become ready for the release. In time, you will feel ready, and it will happen.

Another client created a beautiful ritual to symbolize her release. Rachel planted seeds in her garden. With each seed, she named someone or something to forgive and followed the forgiveness-release process. With water and care, seeds of forgiveness sprouted and grew into plants, and her forgiveness-release felt complete to her.

One other caution about the forgiveness-release process: Many people, myself included, assume that once you have completed your work here, you are finished for life. Think of it like this: You are now an empty bottle or a blank slate. What's the tendency? To fill it up again. This can happen easily and quickly. Some of my clients actually feel panic at this "blank-slate" stage because they realize so much of their identity is wrapped up in the past. If you feel anxious about coming clean, go slowly and gently, and get the support of a friend or counselor as you form a new identity based on your present self.

Recently, I needed to have my car repaired. For years, I had taken it to the same garage. This time I had a bad feeling before I took it in, but I ignored my intuition. That was a mistake. The repairs were expensive, incomplete, and incorrect, and I knew I would have to take it to another garage to be fixed. Every time I got into my car to go somewhere, I was reminded of the mechanic who cost me so much time and money and messed up my car. My hands gripped the steering wheel tightly, my jaw clenched, and my mind was distracted by the situation. Let's face it: When you are driving, the last thing you need is a distraction. Being present helps to avoid accidents. About two weeks later, as my hands tightened up on the steering wheel, again reliving the past perceived injustice, I realized what I was doing. I was letting my energy get caught up in a past event that I needed to release. Right then and there, I did the forgiveness-release process and moved on. I no longer feel upset when I look at or drive my car. I have managed to release and stay present. Remember, just because you clean your house one time, really well, does not mean that you never have to dust again. Keep yourself clean by staying current with your forgiveness-release issues.

I have found that the hardest person to forgive is yourself. Think of your best friend. Got him or her in mind? Now imagine that each time your best friend comes over to visit, or speaks with you, you remind her of something she did twelve years ago. You let her know how stupid it was and how you can't believe she did that. Over and over again, you berate her for this mistake. How long would she want to be your best friend? Yet, this is exactly what we do to ourselves. In our minds, we are filled with self-criticism and negative self-talk. We treat ourselves worse than anyone we know.

Start forgiving yourself for anything that happened in the past. You learned from it. That is enough. Move on. You would let your best friend move on, why not yourself?

THE WRITING ON THE WALL

For many of us, the hardest situation to forgive is an act of betrayal. Can you think of a betrayal in your life? You probably can come up with many: a secret you told someone that wasn't kept, a person in a position of power who used you, a loved one who humiliated you in front of others, a dear friend who lied to you, a love interest who cheated on you, and so on.

For me, and for many people I've worked with, betrayal can be one of our best teachers. It is unfortunate, as the pain of betrayal is so intense. But there is a way to receive the lessons of betrayal without needing to physically manifest the betrayal, either as a life experience or as a lack of health. As you work more and more with your intuition, you will come to a point where you can perceive how a situation will turn out before you enter it, without having to physically experience it. Eventually, you will see the writing on the wall. Or perhaps you will go through the experience in a gentler way because of your greater awareness.

CASE STUDIES

For example, after working with her intuition for only a few months, Esmerelda realized that all of her relationships seemed to end with betrayal. Employment, romance, and friendship all held this pattern for her. With this newer awareness, created by her intuition, she looked at her work situation more clearly and saw all the signals she had not paid attention to: a noncommunicative boss, no performance reviews, no raises, no promotion, and unfriendly co-workers. All of this created an unhealthy work environment. Because Esmerelda's intuitive guidance had been the spark that motivated her to look at the situation more clearly, she checked in with it again. Esmerelda was afraid to move on, but her intuition helped her realize she needed to leave before she experienced a physical betrayal, such as being fired. After resigning, she opened her own company and has enjoyed success ever since.

Fred now knows that when he sees the writing on the wall, he had better pay attention. He felt he needed physical evidence to know that his wife was no longer interested in continuing their relationship. He had dream after dream of his spouse cheating on him, but he did not want to believe it. Eventually, he investigated, validated, and acted on this intuitive information. Many acquaintances—who had been afraid to tell him before the breakup—came forward, confirming his suspicions. Fred was deeply saddened by the end of his relationship; however, he believes that he saved himself much more pain, trouble, and heartache by getting out of the relationship sooner rather than later. He credits his intuition and the courage to follow his hunches for lessening his suffering; in the future, he believes he will be even more aware and willing to act quickly and confidently.

I believe that through listening to your inner guidance, you, too, can see the signs, feel the future as it is unfolding, and take steps to strengthen yourself. In school, if you knew a test was coming up and you studied for it, you probably found it easier to pass than a test for which you had not prepared. The person who studied may think the test was easy, while the person who did not study may think the same exam was a hard one. The same thing is true with life and intuition. Study, prepare, and fortify yourself. Get the message—the health or life lesson—ahead of time. Life will still hold challenges for you, but through your intuition (you'll learn more about this in section 2) and a proactive approach, you will be better able to face these tests and they will seem easier. How? Here's an example: Three years ago, Patricia consulted me for a reading. I suggested some physical treatment modalities for her to explore and some emotional changes she needed to make as well. I told her that if she didn't work on these issues now, I saw an eventual bone density problem in her right leg, especially the right hip. I saw a vision of her as an old lady walking with a cane. Within the last month, Patricia called me. Two years ago, she had a bone density scan. It was normal. She began having problems with her right hip and leg six months ago and insisted that a bone scan be performed on the right hip (in response to my intuitive insights), instead of the customary left hip. Patricia told me, "The bone density of the right hip had decreased nearly 8 percent in two years, while the other areas had a small decrease that is to be expected at my age." Patricia decided to check in with me. We conducted a new reading and reviewed the old reading, which reaffirmed that she needed to pursue the course of working with the emotional components to her hip and right leg problem as well as the therapeutic modalities intuitively suggested, if her doctor agreed. Following this course of action, Patricia is now experiencing relief.

If Patricia had followed my advice earlier, would she have experienced pain and loss of bone in her right hip? Based on my experience with other clients and with Patricia too, I believe so. In the original reading with Patricia I had asked her about leg pain awakening her at night. She confirmed this finding, and I gave her suggestions to alleviate the problem. She followed my advice immediately and experienced complete relief.

Patricia is not the only client with whom I have predicted health problems before they manifested. This reinforces my belief that by using intuition to discover what physical, emotional, mental, and spiritual areas we need to work on, we are learning lessons ahead of time. If you learn these lessons, then there is less likelihood that you will experience a lack of health, because you have already "passed the test." Intuitive insight can help to bring your attention to any emotion or issue, not just betrayal. If you cooperate and listen to your intuition, you will find that life flows more easily.

What health or life issues can be helped by enhancing your energy through divine connection and forgiveness-release? All of them. Results are customized to the individual; there is no generalized response. For example, I can't tell you, "The right elbow is helped by every single person who does this." It may be the right elbow in one person, cancer in another, and depression in a third person. Another person may need to practice divine connection and forgiveness-release in concert with working on other issues in order to experience improvement. I have seen these two techniques help clients with specific physical complaints, or just make them "feel better." Whatever your needs, forgiveness-release and divine connection will help.

As you were reading, did you take note of your feelings about forgiveness-release and divine connection? Based on the criteria I have suggested, do you think these issues are a priority for you, something to work on later, or something that is not a factor? Take a moment to reflect before you read on.

CHAPTER 8

Energy Drains: Situations and People

One of the most interesting phenomena I observe in doing intuitive readings is how drained we become by losing energy to everyday situations and other people. Many of my clients are sensitive individuals. They are saddened by the misfortune they see in their lives, in the lives of their loved ones, and in our world. Many of us feel this way to a certain degree and are adversely affected. This effect can be felt slightly, moderately, or intensely. But it is possible to be sensitive and compassionate without feeling drained.

Grace is a client who has worked hard on many of her issues. She is a well-balanced person who tries to live her life with integrity on all levels. However, when it comes to issues with her family, Grace can be pulled off balance. She has always had a strained relationship with her sister, Ruth. No matter what Grace does or doesn't do, it never seems good enough for Ruth. Ruth leaves messages on Grace's answering machine designed to make Grace feel guilty and undermine Grace's relationships with other family members. She is an expert at pushing Grace's hot buttons and does so often. Every time Grace would hear from her sister, her stomach and jaw would clench up, and she would spend hours saddened and distracted. Although Grace could still function after one of these incidents, the situation would remain in the back of her mind, draining her energy.

BLESS AND RELEASE

Grace was helped by work I had done with another client. Jolene is an extreme example of energy drains. She is a deeply caring individual, but in her case, this caring had turned into something very draining. Although it is a positive thing to be a caring and sensitive person, there is a negative or shadow side to it that can be just as unhealthy as any destructive habit. For Jolene, the most distant signal of tragedy—for example, an ambulance siren in the distance—was extremely upsetting, at times incapacitating. When I did a reading for her, the words *bless and release* came through. Where I lived in Colorado (and probably elsewhere too), some of our fishing areas are designated "catch and release." This means that once you catch a fish, you put it right back in the water to let it live its life. I love the similarity between the slogans "catch and release" and "bless and release"—it makes the phrase easy to remember. Many of my clients and students have been helped by these simple words and the image this phrase evokes. Here is the process:

If a situation or person is upsetting to you, take a moment to quietly send a blessing. You can make up your own blessing, or a simple "bless you" will do. Then hold the intention to release your attachment to the outcome.

Tragedies can be so upsetting that we unconsciously may try to take on the energy of a situation we perceive as negative. Often, we wish a situation's outcome to be different. For example, *Perhaps the accident could have been avoided. I hope the people involved will be okay. I hope there were no children involved.* We have no idea what the overall plan is for people involved in a tragedy. It may be the best way for them to learn a lesson, to become who they need to be—we may never know.

What can you, as a singular person, do? By bestowing a bless and release, you infuse such situations and other people with divine energy, energy that is unlimited and untainted with your attachment to outcome, be it conscious or unconscious. You energize others without draining your own resources. Another important element is that you are not worsening a situation by adding your own feelings to it, which may unnecessarily compound its complexity and lengthen its resolution. This exercise seems to help even the most sensitive of my clients (like Jolene and Grace) and students to avoid taking on extra burdens—a certain drain of their life energy.

Sensitivity encompasses many areas in my clients' lives. Many of them are unaware of their sensitive, intuitive nature. I ask them if they pick up other people's "vibes." How can you tell? Are you having an excellent day and then seem to "catch" a loved one's bad mood? Are malls, cafeterias, and other crowded places overwhelming to you, because you feel so much? How often do you think that someone else's bad mood is your fault? Answering yes to any of these questions means you are intuitively picking up other people's vibes. Many people have always been this way and are unaware that they are not only picking up others' energy, but are holding on to it as well. There is no way we could possibly know what to do with other people's energy and emotions (we have enough trouble knowing what to do with our own), so why would we try to take them on?

Reading someone's vibe—knowing when he or she is upset, sad, joyful, or feeling a certain way—is fine. It is kind to say to our co-worker, "Ray, are you okay?" Caring and reaching out is a wonderful human quality. However, taking on other people's vibes *as our own* is unhealthy.

As one of my wise students suggests, when you feel you are taking on other people's energy, remind yourself, aloud if you need to, "It's not mine, give it back." Both Grace and Jolene have reduced their sensitivity—and energy drains—by learning to bless and release, to give back emotions that are not theirs, and by practicing the following "letting go" exercise.

LETTING GO

How do we release other people's energy? In her audiotape *Awakening Second Sight,*[1] Judith Orloff, M.D., describes an excellent exercise for reading someone's vibe and then letting it go.

When you feel someone's energy coming toward you, breathe it in on the "in" breath. You will still be able to read the vibe (the person is tired, upset, fearful, joyful, and so on), but you are going to let it pass through you, as if you were a pane of glass. Along your spine, two or three inches above your tailbone, there is a spot that is tender on many people. This is the place where that energy can get stuck. On the "out" breath, visualize, feel, or hear the energy you have just taken in as it leaves. You will still be able to "read" the vibe; for example, you will know that your neighbor Stan is having a bad day and can treat him compassionately. That is not a problem; however, you won't have to have a bad day too. You will know that your wife Kathy is upset, but with this process, you will not catch her bad mood and can be supportive instead of contributing to a negative cycle of energy. Kathy may actually pop out of her mood more quickly because she will only have to deal with her own feelings and energy, rather than a situation that is compounded by your reaction.

Nearly every client who picks up other people's vibes assumes that these feelings are directed toward them, or that they are somehow at fault. Remember that old adage about the word *assume?* It makes an *ass* out of *u* and *me*. On this topic, I asked my intuition, "When people pick up vibes that are not their own, and tend to blame themselves, what percentage of the time does it originate from an outside situation that is *not* their fault? For example, when a loved one seems to be having a bad day?"

The answer: "98 percent of the time." Remember this percentage the next time you assume you're at fault, because according to my intuition, chances are you're not. When you assume people are upset because of you, ask them, "Did I do something? Can I help?" If they say no, take them at their word and get on with your life. Do not dwell on the situation, as it takes away from the present moment and drains your energy. With practice, you will develop a sense of detachment, and, in time, you will be able to achieve it more easily. You will still care about others, but you will no longer take on other people's vibes and blame yourself for their moods.

If you're so sensitive that even watching, hearing, or reading the news bothers you, why not take a break from it? Strengthen yourself through the breathe in/breathe out exercise. Then, when you feel more detached and less likely to take on things you can do nothing about, you can go back to the news. If you find yourself upset about a particular story, practice bless and release. Bless and release and the breathing exercise are both simple but powerful—I have even seen them help people overcome panic attacks.

Blessing is a potent energy boost. It works in close proximity to a situation or over a long distance, and it can be considered a form of prayer. Currently, research is available on the effect of long-distance prayer. Larry Dossey, M.D., cites several studies in his book *Healing Words*. One study, conducted at San Francisco General Hospital by cardiologist Randolph Byrd, divided a group of 393 admitted coronary care patients into halves. One half was remembered in prayer by a prayer group; one was not. Patients did not know that they were being prayed for. There were four findings:

> The prayed-for patients differed in several areas: 1. They were five times less likely than the unremembered group to require antibiotics (three patients compared to sixteen patients). 2. They were three times less likely to develop pulmonary edema. . . . (six compared to eighteen patients). 3. None of the prayed-for group required endotracheal intubation, in which an artificial airway is

inserted in the throat and attached to a mechanical ventilator, while twelve in the unremembered group required mechanical ventilatory support. 4. Fewer patients in the prayed-for group died (although this difference was not statistically significant). This study was conducted similarly to the way a new medication would be tested: double blind, with a control group.[2]

Caroline Myss tells a beautiful story about a victim in a car accident that took place during rush hour. The woman died and floated up out of her body, looking down at the scene below. She could hear what the driver of each car behind her was saying. Most were annoyed that she was making them late; however, the fifth car back held an incredible white light of energy that was bouncing up and into her mangled car. She wondered about the light and immediately found herself witnessing the driver of the fifth car—a complete stranger—praying for her. Just then, she received a message that it was not her time and that she should get back into her body. Before doing so, she got the license plate number of the fifth car. After a year of recovering in the hospital, she showed up on the doorstep of the fifth car's driver. When the stranger who had prayed for her opened the door, she handed her a bouquet of flowers and said, "Thank you for your prayers."[3]

Just as it is possible to be affected by someone's good intentions or prayers, it is also possible to pick up negative intentions. Students and clients often ask me if it is feasible to be "psychically attacked." *

---

* Through my work and conversations with others in the field, I know that there are extremely rare, serious cases of possession, but although possession is a scientifically and spiritually documented phenomenon, I cannot stress enough how uncommon possession really is. *Webster's Collegiate Dictionary* defines *possession* as "dominion by something (as an evil spirit, a passion, or an idea)." When an entity (meaning

Can other people or beings drain our energy? I think full-fledged psychic attack is rare, but people who drain our energy to varying degrees are more common. For the most part, I also believe the solution is simple. Sincerely holding the intention or saying a prayer that this person or situation will no longer be able to affect you is oftentimes enough. Because of free will and the tendency to think about the person or situation, you may need to restate the intention on a daily basis. Convenient times to do so are when you awaken or before you go to sleep. The words *attention* and *intention* sound alike. This can help you remember to be mindful about what you give your attention to, as that can interfere with your stated intention. The more you think about someone (giving your attention to a person) the less focused you are on your intention to not let that person affect you. The act of thinking about him or her drains your energy.

BOUNDARIES AND OTHER PEOPLE'S ENERGY

A humorous example of situational or personal energy interfering with someone's intent involved my spiritual mentor, George. He went to the airport to pick up a VIP. This is a predominant part of his job—George jokes that his car knows the way to the airport nearly as well as he does. On the way back, George found himself missing or nearly missing every exit. It seemed that neither his (nor his car's) vast experience in going to the airport was of any help. He even almost missed the exit to his office. George explained to me that the VIP was so used to getting to places on his schedule and in his way, that his focus, or energy field, permeated even George's

---

human or nonhuman) possession is involved, usually the person who is possessed is unaware of it. If you suspect that someone you know is possessed, it is best to consult an expert, such as an exorcist or a shaman.

superconditioned field. Although the VIP's manipulation was probably unintentional (as is the case with most people who drain energy), in the small space of George's car, he filled every moment with distracting, nonstop conversation. I asked George, "What do you do in a case like that?" He said that once he figured out what was going on, he was able to stay focused and centered (processes he had honed through his meditation practice), ignore the VIP, and concentrate on driving. As soon as the VIP left the car, George felt an immediate energy uplift.

Getting focused and centered can help you when you feel like a klutz. Have you noticed that this happens more around certain people? You were fine a minute ago, and now, with your mother-in-law breathing down your neck, you can't even find a spoon in your own kitchen. And when you do, you keep dropping it. Refocus on your breathing. In your mind, say *spoon, spoon, spoon* or the name of the immediate task at hand. Try to get some distance between yourself and the overwhelming field of the other person. Give her the task of cutting up carrots (now is *not* the best time for you to be using a knife!) at the table, for example, while you work on dinner at the opposite counter. Breathe in her energy and release it on the out breath as many times as it takes. This should help dissipate energy drain so that you aren't as affected.

When a spouse, roommate, or co-worker goes on vacation, you sometimes notice that you have more energy and vitality. The difference may be subtle or highly noticeable. I refer to these people as "energy vampires." They drain your energy, but you don't notice it until they leave your environment temporarily. Upon their return, you might start feeling cranky, fatigued, irritated, or some other negative reaction.

Joe and Kelley lived together for five years. When Joe went away on a business trip, Kelley found herself happy, full of energy, and really not missing Joe. She knew she loved him, but as the days went on, she realized that she had not felt this well in at least two years (a health care professional had suggested that she might be suffering from chronic fatigue syndrome). After his business trip, Joe received an offer to house-sit for a friend who would be in Africa for a month. Kelley encouraged him to do so, as she felt this would be an excellent test of her theory that it really was her close proximity to Joe that resulted in her tiredness and depression. After the first week of Joe's house-sitting, Joe and Kelley decided to go on a weekend getaway to a place about three hours from their town. About halfway there, they realized that they had both come to the same conclusion. They turned to one another and said, "I really love you, and I can't live with you." They moved into separate places, and their friendship has deepened; both feel more energetic and happier than they have in years.

If you are chronically tired, consider how a person or a situation (job, club, volunteer position, task, etc.) may be affecting you. If, after a temporary separation, you are sure of their effects, practice the breathe in/breathe out method of energy intake and release to set better boundaries for yourself. Look at your own control mechanisms too. Are you overly invested in how things turn out? Does everything have to be done your way to please you? Your investment in the outcome can be extremely draining. If all else fails, try talking to the person or people involved, perhaps with a mediator or counselor to guide you. Personal boundaries are the subject of many relationship and self-help books—consider consulting these resources to aid in keeping your energy field strong and intact. A healthy and whole energy field not only keeps your energy level strong and consistent, it keeps you from being drained. When you are drained, you are more likely to manifest ill health, and life doesn't seem to flow as well.

My friend Donna experienced this matter in the extreme. Whenever her best friend, Tim, came to town, something went wrong. Donna and Tim had been friends for years. During one of Tim's visits, Donna backed into his car. She is an extremely mindful and careful person, who had never before had a car accident. The next time Tim came to town, he and Donna made elaborate plans to get together at a spot fifteen minutes from where each was located. Three hours, much stress, and several miscommunications later, they finally met. Visit after visit, there was always a similar situation. Donna's husband, Charles, mentioned to her that when Tim was around, she wasn't herself. She would make excuses for the situations that only seemed to arise when Tim was in town. However, she readily admitted something weird was going on with the string of Tim-related mishaps. Donna and Charles agreed that the next visit would be a test: if another peculiar situation transpired, something would have to be done.

Charles was making dinner when he heard the loud crash that shook the house. Racing out, he found that mindful and careful Donna had rammed the car into the side of the house, with Tim as a passenger. Charles was surprised at the way Donna was acting and speaking—he'd never seen her behave in this way. "Oh, that's too bad," she said, "silly me, I'm a very poor driver."

After Tim left town, Donna and Charles talked. It was clear that her demeanor around Tim was completely unlike her normal conduct. Not only that, she seemed to be unable to think clearly, causing accidents and mishearing conversations. For many months, Donna had been troubled by the way Tim lived his life. He was a "drama king," repeating dysfunctional patterns with people and situations. Tim knew better. He was a trained guidance counselor and freely admitted that his life was out of control and that he did not want to take charge. Sooner or later, friends dropped away from Tim as they grew tired of being caught up in crisis after crisis or trying to help. Donna decided to talk to Tim about how his out-of-control lifestyle and thinking were affecting not only his quality of life but his friends as well. Donna decided that Tim could certainly visit in the future, as she valued their friendship; however, it was not fair to impinge this energy drain on her husband and family. Tim was able to hear his friend's care and compassion and promised to work toward change.

As a last resort, a few of my clients have completely disassociated from people or situations that they can no longer deal with or that may never change. This is a personal decision, made after careful consideration and trying many options, including therapy or mediation. Sometimes it's time to get on with our lives, to learn from a situation that we are unable to transcend, and to move forward. Whatever route you take with people and situations that drain your energy—bless and release, focusing on your breathing, distancing yourself from the situation, or some other practice—remember to keep your attention focused and your intention clear, so that you can make decisions with clarity and work toward rebalancing your life.

CHAPTER 9

Balance

Being in balance is the single most important intention you can set for yourself to attain a healthful and satisfying life. Learn to listen to yourself and do what you need to in order to find your place of equilibrium. Balance is all-encompassing, as it applies to the four levels of health: physical, mental, emotional, and spiritual. For many people, balancing on one foot for an extended period of time is challenging. The same concept applies in our bodies. Not getting enough of something for the self—be it self-nurturing, love, alone time, creativity—is a potent form of imbalance. Rebalancing your life will often lead to improved health, greater energy, and increased satisfaction.

It is hard to create balance in our lives if we continually focus on what other people should be doing. "If they would only listen to me!" is a familiar phrase for the person who wants to "fix" others.

Many times a parent will call me for a reading on herself and her child, sometimes one who is already well into adulthood. I do not read for a fully functioning adult and then give that information to another person, even if it is a relative. I understand that the parent just wants to help the child, but the very private nature of the information contained in a reading is not appropriate for me to share with others. In these cases, the issue of control usually comes up in a major way during the parent's reading. Not every parent is like this, but this "rescuer" or "fixer" pattern is prevalent enough to mention—and it's not exclusive to parents. A rescuer is anyone who tries to fix someone else's life. To be honest, everyone is a fixer to some extent, sometimes, but can you think of one time that you successfully fixed another person's life? No. It is an illusion. People fix their own lives. You can support, suggest, and guide, if you are asked, but no real fixing ever occurs. This is another potent form of energy drain, one in which much time is spent thinking and wishing other people could be different, changed, or healed. And in the end, you are frustrated that these people cannot see that you are "right."

Pam, a devoted mother, asked me to do a reading on her grown daughter, Leslie. Pam felt Leslie needed a reading, but she would not pursue one herself. Pam wanted me to share the information I obtained with her, instead of with Leslie. I received the impression that the daughter could not benefit from an intuitive consultation at this time in her life. It was the mother who needed the reading. A good portion of our hour together was spent explaining to her that she could not fix anyone, including Leslie. The outcome Pam was projecting was her own ideal, and it probably had little to do with the divine plan that was in place for her daughter. She finally agreed that this concept made sense. Pam realized that she was pouring all her energy into an attachment to outcome: she was wishing for a certain type of cure for her daughter. She was actually contributing to an unhealthy atmosphere with these projections. Pam needed to see herself as more than a mother—as a whole person who needed to learn to focus on herself. Her top priority was to stop putting other people's needs first in place of her own.

Putting others first at the extreme cost to the self is what I call being a martyr. When I work with my clients and the martyr pattern comes up as a prominent issue in their lives, I always ask, "Do you know what a martyr is?" One client replied (only half-jokingly), "A martyr is a mother! That's why the words sound alike!" I do see the martyr behavior in a lot of mothers, but it can happen in any situation. *Webster's New World Dictionary* defines a *martyr* as someone "who chooses to suffer or die rather than give up their faith or principles . . . a person who suffers great pain or misery for a long time . . . a person who assumes an attitude of self-sacrifice or suffering in order to arouse feelings of pity, guilt, etc." Some or all of these issues can be found in a person who possesses the martyr pattern. Can you think of someone you know who continually puts others first and suffers silently (or loudly) because of it—even though they could choose another course? Perhaps there are times when you have done the same.

CONSIDER YOURSELF FIRST

Although we can logically see that being a martyr is unnecessary and detrimental to health and well-being, why do we do it? I believe this behavior is programmed into many of us during childhood with the admonishment "Don't be self-centered!" Take a moment to look at the term *self-centered*. Break it into two: *self* and *centered*. These are two very good things to be: yourself (knowing the self) and centered (balanced). Why would we be told differently? Control plays a role here too. If you are not in charge of yourself, or you are off balance and cannot freely think for yourself, another person can more easily control you. Many people unintentionally use the "Don't be self-centered" admonishment to control others. Just as unknowingly, people are controlled by it. Admonishments and behaviors of this sort are traditionally learned, passed down from one generation to the next. The following analogies illustrate the need to consider putting the self first.

Do you know what organ the heart pumps blood to first? Think a minute before you continue to read. Many of my clients and students guess the lungs, the liver, the brain, the stomach, and so on. The heart pumps blood to *itself* first. Our physical bodies provide us with a primary example to use as inspiration.

The second analogy provides a different perspective. Imagine a glass full of water, overflowing. This represents the amount of energy you have to live your life. When a glass is overflowing, and you have had plenty to drink, it is easy to use discernment and offer a sip to others in need. Now imagine the glass half-full, or nearly bone dry, with only a drop to spare. You are parched with thirst and really need to drink a full glass to quench your thirst and clear your mind. If you are very thirsty and are still offering water to others first, you are a martyr. Eventually, you become dehydrated, or burned out. You can help no one, not even yourself. By taking care of yourself first, you ensure that your glass is always overflowing, that you have the ability to decide who gets a sip and who does not, as you are not too depleted to choose wisely. You can help those in need when appropriate, at no adverse cost to yourself, your health, or your life. Everybody wins by getting what they need.

Not considering oneself first and lacking self-nurturing and self-love are the most common issues I see in people with unhealthy breast tissue. If you recognize this pattern in yourself, work to change it. Certainly, breast cancer is a hot topic for women as of this writing, but I predict an increase of breast cancer in men. Why? In the Western world, more men are becoming single fathers. They find themselves having to do it all: trying to fill the mother role while holding down a full-time job. Without the support of a partner, they have learned to put all of their needs last and to criticize themselves for not being able to do everything for everyone. Whether or not you are a parent, Dr. Wayne Dyer's classic, *Your Erroneous Zones*,[1] is a wonderful resource to learn about self-love. Ask for help from others —you do not have to do this alone.

Many times, I'll ask a client, "Do you love yourself?"

"I do!" is the emphatic reply.

"Intuitively, I am getting the impression that you think your calves are too large; they remind you of your mother's calves and you feel people are staring at them all the time."

"Well, I don't like my calves, but I love all of me." As my client says the words aloud, she starts to see that loving herself means loving the *total* self, calves and all.

One way to get out of the habit of not liking parts of yourself—or of being hard on yourself, full of negative self-talk and self-criticism—is to treat yourself as your own best friend, as I suggested earlier when talking about self-forgiveness. You would not tolerate this type of behavior toward any dear friend of yours—why would you allow this to happen to you? Be your own best friend. Treat yourself with kindness, gentleness, love, and forgiveness.

When I ask my clients what they do for self-nurturing, these are some typical responses:

"I take the kids [or dog] for a walk."

"I get a facial, so I can stay young looking [so my spouse won't leave me for a younger woman]."

"I take a bath [not for relaxation, but because I'm dirty]."

"I go to the gym [I might be able to meet someone if I look good]."

I get similar responses when I ask about their creative outlets:

"Yard work."

"At work, I sometimes get to draw."

"Reading the newspaper."

How do you know if you are performing an act of self-nurturing? Look at your motivations. Facials and massages are wonderful, if you are doing it for *you*, not to get or keep a partner. Going to the gym for your health and well-being, not because you care what other people think, is fine. Connecting with nature while working in your garden can be a wonderful form of divine connection as well as an expression of creativity. Are you doing yard work because you love it, or because you have to? We all do tasks we don't like—it's part of being an adult. But try to integrate some activities you love in your day, to show yourself the value you place on you.

Self-nurturing and creative expression are needed for balance in our lives. Balance is the key to everything in life and, subsequently, in health. Many times I see poor nutrition in people who do not value themselves. Unconsciously, they send the message to their bodies, "You are not worth good food." This is an expression of lack of self-worth. Eating good and tasteful foods, consistently and moderately, can be an important expression of self-value and self-nurturing, as well as an important health practice.

LISTENING TO YOURSELF

One of the best gifts we can give ourselves is to listen. Listen to your inner voice. Although I will be teaching you more about how to do this in section 2, I want to bring the importance of this practice to your attention now. How many times have you promised yourself one thing, only to do another?

"I'll start that diet on New Year's Day."

"This summer, I'm going to get in shape with an exercise program."

Later, you may say to yourself:

"Well, I didn't say *this* New Year's."

"There are too many other things to do this summer."

You didn't keep your commitment, but at what cost to yourself? More than losing out on the healthy benefits of diet and exercise, you have lied to yourself. One of the most important things I've learned is this: If you can't trust yourself, whom can you trust? The answer is no one. Many people have concerns around trusting others. Maybe you have trust issues with a certain profession. For example, some people have had bad experiences with a lawyer or a car salesperson. They then decide they cannot rely on any of them. In the past, a boss or co-worker may have betrayed you. Now you are suspicious of everyone you work with, even though you may have changed jobs. Or, on a more personal level, you may believe all potential love interests are untrustworthy. You are then unable to experience a fulfilling relationship. I will tell you the best relationship secret I know: learn to trust yourself. Once you attain a satisfying, trusting relationship with yourself, you can experience it with others too.

How do you learn to trust yourself? Listen to that little voice in your head, that vision that flashes in your mind's eye, or that funny feeling. Think about all the times you did not pay attention. Are you glad or are you sorry? If the answer is the latter, start listening now. Then you can start in small ways to act on the information, as I will explain in greater detail in section 2. If you had a friend that you walked away from every time he or she offered you guidance, would that friend want to stick around? You at least give your friend the courtesy of listening.

Think about the way you cultivate a new friendship: slowly and cautiously. Your intuition may be like that shy new friend, and you may need time to cultivate it. Learn to trust yourself. It is the best message you can give to yourself. Other people will always disappoint you. That does not mean they are bad or wrong. It means they are doing what they think is best, which may not necessarily be the same as what you wish. You will never disappoint yourself if you make the vow to trust, and listen to, yourself. You may not always act on your intuitive knowing, but at least listen to it and then decide. Cultivate your relationship with yourself—it is the best gift to give to you, and you alone can give it.

ALONE TIME

Taking a walk alone, just for you, is a wonderful present to give yourself. I recently heard a survey on the radio regarding free time. The survey asked people, "If you could choose what to do with your free time, what would you do?" Only 13 percent would choose to spend it with their families; the rest wanted time alone. I was not surprised. Lack of alone time, especially for adults with children, careers, or both, is a predominant theme in the readings. We all need alone time. Until very recently, we were a mostly agrarian society. Long hours alone in the field, working the crops, gave us plenty of time to think and contemplate. Our population has grown; industrialization is now the norm. Alone time is a precious commodity and much needed for balance.

How can you get it? Even if you wake up just fifteen minutes earlier every day to walk, meditate, or read, you are giving yourself consistent, daily alone time that you never had before. It sets the tone for your entire day and can ease resentment and feelings of being overwhelmed. Be creative. Where I live, you can hire a grocery-shopping service for ten dollars a week—not per hour, per week. Would you pay ten dollars to get alone time that you would be spending going to the market? Delegate the grocery shopping, or the cleaning, or the yard work. Hire a neighborhood kid to help you out. If they do it a little differently than you would, so what? You saved five hours or more! Plus, you are learning to allow. Perfect. Keep track on a pad of paper how much TV you watch during the day. Every single minute counts. Add it up at the end of the week—the hours consumed can be surprising. Invest some of that time in yourself instead. Even if you feel too tired to do anything but watch TV, just sit still, quiet your mind, contemplate, or reflect. An amazing thing happens. Without even trying, you have just started a regular meditation practice.

CREATIVE EXPRESSION

With the extra time you have found or saved, you will have space for creative expression. You are a fertile individual. Heavy workloads and responsibilities, along with a de-emphasis on art curricula in school systems, may be leaving one side of your brain primarily unused. Roger Sperry's groundbreaking work on split-brain research, begun in the 1950s, won him the Nobel Prize in 1981. He proved that the right side of the brain is the seat of our nonverbal functioning. Based on Sperry's work, the best-selling book *Drawing on the Right Side of the Brain*[2] by Betty Edwards offers a program to enhance artistic ability and confidence. Many people feel that intuition resides in the right side of the brain. You have a whole brain, not half a brain. Even if you feel you have no talent for painting, singing, gardening, writing, or intuition, by exploring your creative interests, you will be incorporating the use of your right brain.

I have found that as my work in intuition has intensified, my artistic skill has manifested. Let me assure you, there were absolutely no signs of artistic ability before—people winced when they looked at my "art," and I just could not seem to express what I wanted. As my intuition increased in my thirties, I started watercolor painting. I paid attention to the expression and the process, *not* the outcome. Whatever came, came, and I decided not to judge. My resolve of nonjudgment did not hold, as I think my paintings are beautiful! I love to see the expression on people's faces when I show them my watercolors. Those who are familiar with my former efforts respond with a mixture of confusion and amazement. What's more, my creativity *flows*. It comes out of me easily, where before it was work, work, work, and disappointment. Many of my clients find that incorporating regular creative time into their week—through classes, books, videos, or alone time—has become a form of meditation and spiritual practice. They gain energy, calmness, and clarity from it. They release anger, resentment, and other unproductive feelings and attitudes.

Creative expression comes in many forms. It can be artistic, such as drawing, painting, or making pottery. Many of my clients like the childlike messiness of working with clay—and having someone else at the pottery studio take care of cleaning up. Others like the earthy feeling of working with dirt in the garden. Even city dwellers can have a window box or potted plants to express their gardener's heart. Many towns have community gardens that you can rent for a small fee or, even better, volunteer gardens that grow food for those less fortunate. Music can be a creative endeavor—playing it, listening to it, dancing, or singing. Clients clench up when I bring up these types of outlets. I am not suggesting a performance recital, merely some private time expressing your artistic side. Sing along with the radio in the car. Or roll up the rug, pull down the window shades, and dance!

One of my clients, Audrey, is a talented painter. She exhibits her work in galleries the world over. However, when it comes to singing, she is anything but public—she is terrified. But the idea of chanting thrills her. So, by herself, she is exploring chanting along to recorded music—and she loves it.

Some of my clients tell me, "I am not creative or innovative in the least. Not everyone is, you know!" The culinary arts—cooking, baking, decorating—can be a relaxing expression of creative flow, and then you are rewarded by getting to eat your efforts. The written word—in journaling, poetry, fiction, even correspondence—is another way to let your fertile creative energy flow. Volunteering in a community—building or repairing homes, mentoring others, teaching—can be fulfilling, balancing, and rewarding. People get stuck on the word *creativity*. They think it means they have to have some artistic talent (for example, the ability to paint or play the flute) or be good at creating to enjoy it. Not so. Creative expression is anything, done on a regular basis, that helps you express yourself, whether it's a hobby, like woodworking, or just sitting around sharing ideas with others.

Just to show you how limitless innovation and creation can be, I will share a couple of stories about a couple of nonhumans—my dogs. Shelby, my older Newfoundland, has invented a way to get all the bones from the other dogs. She pretends she sees a squirrel, runs off in that direction, and stops as soon as the other dogs start chasing the imaginary prey. While they are looking hard for their quarry, Shelby picks up all their bones in her mouth, puts them in a pile, and lies on top of them. The dogs come back from their hunt and cannot figure out where their bones are.

Blaize, another of my Newfoundlands, has found a way to share fresh watermelon with the other dogs. She simply knocks the whole melon off the counter and lets it break open from the fall. One by one, she takes a piece outside to share with each dog, and then comes back in to get her own. Creativity can be expressed as a new way of doing things. Now that you know how creative the animal kingdom—at least in my backyard—can be, you might not have any excuses left for not finding your own creative expression. Why not try it? To manifest greater wholeness and well-being, find time for the fertile balance in your life.

MEDITATION

As I mentioned earlier, in my story about the artist's model and her chakras, meditation is a wonderful way to synchronize your energy system, and the physical effects are well documented. C. Norman Shealy, M.D., Ph.D., in his book *The Self-Healing Workbook*, lists the following benefits derived from relaxation: "decreased blood pressure; slower, more regular heart rate; decreased muscle tension; decreased insulin requirement; decreased adrenal production."[3]

There are many different terms for meditation, such as *focused relaxation*, *the empty mind*, or, in the Christian tradition, *contemplative prayer*. Whatever you call it, meditation is a time to clear your brain, slow down your life, and listen to any inner messages that come through from the right brain, the intuitive (and artistic) side. Intuition is like a gentle breeze on a summer's day—if you aren't paying attention to it, you'll miss it. A quiet mind does wonders for opening up this right-brain function, giving it expression, and adding balance to your life.

EXERCISE

Exercise is another wonderful way to rebalance your life. *Gentle, consistent*, and *moderate* are the words that most often come through in regard to exercise in my readings, and walking is at the top of the list. Start daily, first thing in the morning, before your day gets away from you. Once around the block. That's it. Easy. You can do it. Every day. Pretty soon, you might want to add more—or maybe not—you decide. Recently, I did a reading on a woman in her late sixties. Marjorie had the most beautiful knees I had seen in a long time. (Remember, I conduct readings long-distance, and I see with my intuition.) I said to her, "Either you've had your knees replaced, or

you've been doing some consistent form of exercise, probably walking." She told me that she had sold her car and walked everywhere,
about two miles a day. Study after study touts the benefits of walking, but for some reason—maybe because it's too easy or because we
hear about it too much—we tune out and neglect something that is
available to nearly every one of us.

However, if walking does not appeal to you, don't do it. It has been
my experience in guiding people intuitively that if they dislike a certain type of exercise, they will only add negativity to their lives if they
force themselves to do it. So, when I tune in, I ask which exercise is
best for my client. (In section 2, you will learn how to tune in and get
this answer for yourself.) I intuitively choose and suggest one or more
types of exercise that would be good for my client's body. If the person enjoys the activity, the effect is more than physical well-being; it
also positively affects the mind and the spirit. Gentle types of exercise are most often recommended: stretching and breathing (such as
yoga) and walking. Sometimes I suggest swimming, hiking, Pilates
(a form of strengthening and stretching created by Joe Pilates), and
martial arts. Although martial arts are not generally thought of as
gentle, some forms, such as tai chi and chi kung, are. Additionally,
some of the more defensive forms of martial arts enhance one's sense
of personal safety. Whatever kind of exercise appeals to you, try it
and see what unfolds.

A balanced life is a wonderful gift to give to yourself. It doesn't
take as much time as you might think, and the benefits are endless.

As you were reading this chapter, did you remember to check in
and see how you felt about each of these areas? Were you irritated,
annoyed, or angry as you read the paragraphs on exercise? Alone
time? Something else? If so, examine that area more closely. These
feelings usually mean this is a priority. If you felt sleepy or cannot
remember what you just read, chances are this is an even bigger issue
for you and you might want to work through other priorities first,

then this one. Finally, a neutral interest while reading this chapter indicates that you may not need to focus a great deal on this area.

Remember the key words: *gentle*, *consistent*, and *moderate*. Take small steps as you work toward a balanced life, whether by learning to put yourself first, giving yourself the self-love and nurturance you need, making sure you have alone time, expressing yourself creatively, or allowing quiet time through meditation and exercise.

CHAPTER 10

Emotional and Behavioral Issues

This chapter covers a lot of ground: worry, guilt, fear, control, judgment, anger, and depression. After each topic, stop and do the self-test. Are you irritated, angry, or annoyed? This might be a good issue to focus on now. Are you sleepy and unable to remember what you just read? Work on this later. Do you feel neutral? Congratulations, you've probably worked through this issue. Take this chapter slowly—remember, baby steps—and don't be hard on yourself. Read about these emotional issues with the idea that learning is the first step—and sometimes the biggest one.

Guilt, worry, and their various manifestations, such as control—banish them. Why? Because they are useless. I have never seen them help anyone. Although I get a lot of information on such issues from doing readings (you'll see examples of actual readings in section 2), one of the best resources I have found to deal with common, everyday issues is Wayne Dyer's *Your Erroneous Zones*. It includes a wealth of commonsense information on many issues, including worry.

WORRY

Ask yourself this: "When did worry ever help anything?" Dyer says that when you worry, you are thinking about future events that may or may not happen—you are not living in the present moment. He uses the extreme example of the Civil War to demonstrate this. Even with thirty-two million people genuinely worrying about terrible possibilities, the war was not prevented. I have found through reading people that worry can actually contribute a negative outcome, making a situation worse instead of better. It's a definite drain on the system, as we could be spending that time in the now—healing, learning, loving, or doing anything else—but instead, we send out negative worry thought forms to ourselves and others. Dyer counsels us to remember that worry is not love. "I am worried about you" is not the same as "I love you."[1] I have found that people who worry are trying to control others or the outcome of a situation. And, since we know that control doesn't really work, we know that worry doesn't, either.

How do you break the worry habit? Appeal to your logical side with the reasons you have just read, then substitute more positive behavior. If you need your awareness brought to the forefront, simply hold the intention that you will notice every time you worry. Years ago, I heard a self-help tape that suggested wearing a rubber band around your wrist. Every time a negative thought came into your head, you were to snap yourself with the band. I think that's a little harsh—and you might end up with a big red welt before too long. However, any harmless tool that you think would help you keep track of how much time is devoted to worry, so that you can shift out of it, might be worth trying. For example, you could try writing your worries in a notebook or on a worry chart on the wall, or speaking them aloud.

One of the biggest worries people have is about money. Often, this worry can lead to acute problems in the pelvic area (including the low back), although it manifests itself elsewhere as well. Because money is such a large subject and an important issue for people, I refer my clients to appropriate resources. This way, we can spend most of our time covering their overall health, and they can delve deeply into particular issues (like money) on their own. Two of my favorite financial resources are *The Energy of Money*,[2] an audiotape by Maria Nemeth, and *The 9 Steps to Financial Freedom*,[3] a book by Suze

Orman. Nemeth's tape covers common issues. Be aware when you "zone out" and miss part of what she is saying. If you have to rewind several times, this can indicate a big issue. Orman's book demystifies many common money terms and ideas. If you start skipping over some content or find yourself daydreaming elsewhere when you read about a certain topic, that's a key area for work. Perhaps work on the issues that annoy or anger you first, then hit the bigger ones.

GUILT

The opposite of worry is guilt. Why? Worry helps you avoid the present by spending time in the future; guilt lets you wallow in the past. You are best served by being present. Having all your energy at your fingertips to live your life, make decisions, and work toward optimum health necessitates being in the present moment.

Guilt can be about control. You are easier to control if you are susceptible to guilt: "If you don't come over for Thanksgiving, you'll ruin the day for everyone." "What do you mean you won't work late? Everyone else does." "If you really loved me, you would _____" (fill in the blank).

The Roman Catholic Church is a historical example of guilt in action. During the Middle Ages and into the Renaissance, the church sold indulgences. This was a way to pay for your sins now, so that you could go to heaven later. One could even buy indulgences for sinful people who had already died. Although indulgences are no longer offered, the tradition of "I must pay for my sins" continues to the present day in some organized religions. When I read for people who have heavy guilt issues, they often come from a family tradition that says "I must pay for my sins." I am not condemning organized religion; this is only one example. I am simply saying that if you find that guilt is a big influence in your life, instead of focusing just on one person who uses guilt on you, also look to that person's background. Where did that person learn to use guilt? It was probably "handed down" by another person or an organization. Why do you let others use guilt on you? The answer may lie in your background too.

We all learn from our mistakes. Learn from them and go on. You do not need to feel guilty or let others goad you with guilt in order to be a better person. Going back to the past over and over again after you've already learned from it drains you of energy and keeps you from putting your best effort into the present. We are human. We make mistakes. We learn from them. Forgive yourself and free yourself from guilt. Transcending guilt is similar to working through worry. Ask yourself: "What am I avoiding in the present by staying in the past?" "When did guilt ever change anything?" "Who or what is getting my energy through guilt?"

LIVING IN THE PRESENT

Why do we spend most of our time away from the present? Intuitively, I have received this answer: because we think that the future costs nothing; it hasn't happened yet. It's the present and the past that cost us. As I've explained in other chapters, continued focus on our past mistakes, people we haven't forgiven, and so on, can drain our energy. How does the present cost us? It takes energy to live in the present; it is what is happening now; it is our reality. Many of us spend our time in the future, because we think that it is free—that there is no cost to something that is not real. We escape reality through habits such as daydreaming, fantasizing, and worrying about what may or may not happen. What seems to cost nothing actually does cost something, or even a lot (depending on how much time we spend on these habits). By spending time in the future, we expend precious energy. We need as much of our energy in the now, in the present, as we can muster. It gives us greater clarity for making decisions, and the more energy we have in the present, the better we feel, the greater our well-being, and the more strength we will have to deal with the ups and downs of life, especially the downs—life's tragedies and fears.

FEAR

What are we afraid of? So many things. Earlier I mentioned that the biggest fear I see in people is the fear of being alone. Overall, nearly every fear fits into this category: "What if something bad happens?" This is also a worry (future concern). Worry and guilt are partners with control. Worry is about us wanting to control the future; guilt is about us wanting to control (change) the past. Let me ask you this: Because you are so good at controlling things, has nothing bad ever happened to you? Consider for a moment before reading further.

Where I lived in Colorado, many people go river rafting. As you prepare to go out on the river, the guides tell you what to do if you fall out of the boat. Most people try to grab on to a rock, a floating log, or branches overhanging the river. If you hold on tightly to something, you will get beaten up by the river and possibly knocked unconscious or drowned. The river guides say that if you can tell which way is downstream, point your feet in that direction. Regardless, you are to *go with the flow*. Likewise, how do we surpass or transcend control? By realizing it does not work. By reminding ourselves, even if we have to say it one hundred times a day, "Go with the flow." Remember all the times you have been lost and unable to find an address, but eventually you found it? Or you were delayed, and it turned out to be for the best? One of the best stress-beaters I know is the phrase "Everything is happening as it should." Say it over and over again when you are in a stressful situation. You'll notice your hands relaxing, your breath deepening, your jaw unclenching. Put little yellow "sticky notes" all over your house to remind you that "Everything is happening as it should" and "Go with the flow."

As you let go of control, you start to see the fears that have been motivating you. You see that your decisions are not really your own; you have a silent but deadly partner—fear. Maggie, a client of mine, is wheelchair-bound with a progressive neuromuscular condition. As her reading progressed, we talked about her biggest fear. She believed that her husband and two sons would be killed in a hunting accident. She had no intuitive impression of this; it was simply a fear that occupied her mind almost constantly. How did she work through this? Together, we looked the fear full in the face. I have found this to be the simplest and best tactic to get through fear (which can often manifest through worry and guilt). Fear has power over us because we look at it out of the corners of our eyes; we have a vague idea of the fear, but we never look at it specifically and completely. Even logically, many fears seem absurd or crazy, but they still have control over us. In Maggie's case, I said, "Okay, so your husband and sons die in a hunting accident. What is your fear underneath that?"

"That there will be no one to take care of me," Maggie said.

"Do you have life insurance on them?"

"Sure," said Maggie. "About a million dollars."

"Could you pay someone to take care of you with a million dollars?"

"Yes. Yes, I could. Not only that," she said, "but they wouldn't give me a hard time, or resent me for it. They would be my employee, and I would be their focus."

The more Maggie talked about it, the more she realized that, yes, she would grieve if her husband and sons died, but she would *survive*. Maybe she would hire help, a relative would step in, or some other scenario would evolve to take care of her. Maggie knew she had the resources to survive. What's most important is that she is no longer paralyzed with fear, and she experienced relief.

The shadow side of fear is shown when we let it control us. Looking deeply at it, knowing what is real about it and why it motivates us, puts us back in partnership with fear. Why "partnership"? Because fear can be a guide. It helps us find our issues, and it can tell us when to be aware, so that we can be safe. We've all experienced this. Can you remember a time when a prickling on the back of your neck while walking alone down a street alerted you to danger? Find your fears. Don't judge yourself for having them—everyone does. Learn from them and work with them.

JUDGMENT

Often, people who carry a lot of guilt are cursing themselves with unkind self-judgment. This is a difficult issue, as many of us judge constantly, without being aware of it. There are many things we need to make judgments about every day, such as stopping at a yellow stoplight instead of driving through it, or making an important decision. There are other times when it is unnecessary. For example, using our judgment to ridicule others or to label a situation as good or bad takes away from the present moment and uses our precious energy. How do we get out of the judging mind habit? First, recognize when you are making an unnecessary judgment. Have you ever been in your car, or standing in a line, and been cut off? You think to yourself, *That jerk!* Perhaps you boil about it for a few seconds or minutes. Was that necessary? Did it help anything? Do you feel better? Perhaps you feel worse, because you are adding a negative judgment to your negative feelings. Those are the types of judgments to let go of.

Spiritual teacher and author Ram Dass has a great method for getting out of the judging mind habit. He suggests that whenever you catch yourself making an unnecessary judgment, you say, "That's true of me too."[4] How many times have you unconsciously acted in a similar way? Thank goodness the other person was watching when you accidentally cut him off in your car, so that no one was injured. Once you think, *That's true of me too*, you shift out of the judging mind. It puts you on par with the rest of humanity and brings compassion into the picture, replacing whatever negative emotions you were feeling with positive ones.

For those of us who guilt ourselves with self-judgment, remember the forgiveness process. We can only be guilty about the past, because the future has not happened. So, to release your energy from the past, do the three-step forgiveness-release process from chapter 7 (it happened in the past, I learned from it, and I'm ready to let go). Realize that you are being hard on yourself. Most people who feel a lot of guilt and who negatively judge themselves are trying to measure up to a standard of perfection. You are not a god, you are human. You will not ever be perfect. Forgive yourself. To help you shift away from this unhealthy standard that you hold yourself to, reverse Ram Dass's statement. Instead, say, "That's true of them too." This will remind you that with six billion people (and counting) on our planet, someone, somewhere, at one time or another, did just what you did. It reminds you that you are part of the human family and helps you to ease up on yourself, knowing that you are not alone in your perceived failings. Others have learned from the same kinds of trials and tribulations. Release yourself with compassion by saying, "That's true of them too."

DEFENSE ISSUES

When we become angry with ourselves and others, it's often as a result of some of the issues I have discussed: control, guilt, worry, lack of time or creative expression, improper diet, and lack of exercise. When people have certain sensitivities to food, it has been my experience that they can undergo intense mood swings (fly into a rage easily, become incredibly sad in a moment, have a huge drop in energy, etc.). It is as if they have taken a drug. It is important to identify the causative agents of food sensitivities and to work to eliminate or clear them from the system on a physical as well as an emotional level. The number-one pattern I see in people with sensitivities (to food, environment, people, etc.) and allergies is the issue of defense. This shows itself in many ways: feeling unsafe in the world; feeling unable to defend oneself; feeling attacked (or about to be); believing the best defense is a good offense—the manifestations are endless. How do we deal with a serious emotional issue around defense? Often in the readings, short-term counseling is suggested. On a physical level, martial arts. Think of it in terms of trickle-down effects: you work to enhance your physical skills and energy field through the study of martial arts, and your emotional self becomes more confident with your newfound abilities. If the martial arts do not resonate for you, see what else appeals. Some other options may include working with a friend or a counselor around fear issues and boundaries or talking to local safety officials about what precautions you can take. My favorite books on fear and safety are *The Gift of Fear*[5] and *Protecting the Gift*,[6] both by Gavin de Becker.

ANGER

The more you work on self-forgiveness, the more even-keeled you become. Resentment, regret, and bitterness all come under the guise of anger. As you release (as I discussed in chapter 7), you have fewer issues pushing at you from the past, whether self-made or taken on from others. As you become more clear, you'll be able to deal with things in a calmer manner. As you release and express, you'll be capable of moving on more quickly. As Caroline Myss says, "You can be bitter, or you can get better."[7]

Appropriate expression of anger is important. It's not something we are often taught. So if you need to garner some skills, invest in a counseling session with a therapist who is comfortable dealing practically with anger and confrontation issues. If you don't feel you need that level of support, there are many books, tapes, and seminars on the subject. Conflict and confrontation are other areas in which we are often left to feel our way in the dark. As a result, we are uncomfortable with them, which can cause anger to build up. If we learn the skills to deal with anger and conflict, we can lessen the anger.

If you give yourself a hard time about your anger, you are only making it worse. We are all working on ourselves, and we are sure to find distasteful aspects in the process. This does not make us bad people, and yet, we say things such as:

"I shouldn't feel this way."

"I hate myself for being so angry."

"I should be a better person and love everyone equally."

In the self-help field, criticizing yourself in this manner is called "shoulding." When you "should" on yourself and criticize your true feelings, you only compound the problem. Instead, acknowledge that your true feeling is anger and stop there. Many times this helps to diffuse the situation, clear your mind, and allow a quicker solution or release.

If you have been lying to yourself (remember the discussion in chapter 9 about broken promises to yourself?), much of the anger may originate there. Examine the situation closely and see if you can take this component out of the mix. Take a deep breath in, and let it out slowly. Count to ten if you like. Pause and think, *What is really going on here?* Take a moment to examine what's upsetting you, and then look further behind each reason that comes up—get to the root of the issue, if you can. Look at your deeper motivations, then respond. Because you have postponed your anger for a few moments and taken a deeper look, you might find yourself responding in an improved way—one that is more congruent with your true self and feelings.

Look also at the self-love factor. Again, if you berate yourself when you find your actions distasteful, you are sending a negative message to the self. You are not loving all of yourself. You can love all of yourself and still want to improve and shift, but the more anger and hate you send toward the self, the worse it feels. If you yelled at a child, an animal, or a friend for the way they truly felt, bad or good, how would they react? Would they be sullen? Angry? Uptight? Ready to blow up? Think about what you are doing to yourself by getting upset on top of your anger. Loving yourself even when you are angry helps to send a positive message to others and to yourself.

MEDITATION

Often, it is hard to think or act clearly and rationally when we are angry. We feel that if we could just clear our heads, we could get past the anger or do something constructive about it. The suggestions I have just made will help you get there. But if you truly want to be able to stay calm and balanced in the center of the storm—whether it be caused by anger, worry, control, guilt, judgment, or any of the other negative emotions—you might consider cultivating a meditation practice. Focused, relaxed attention for a few minutes each day can make a great difference in physical health. I often suggest the image of a buoy when I am reading for a client. Think of how this floating marker stays anchored and centered, even in the midst of an angry sea or a severe storm. It bounces to and fro, at times bending almost horizontally, but it never comes off its true center. Meditation and relaxation can help you be like a buoy: no matter what comes up, you will be better able to weather the storm and stay anchored and centered.

Through my work, I have seen meditation-relaxation practices declutter the mind and expand time. Our brains are so saturated these days. We live in a fast-paced society full of information. Think of how much better and clearer you feel after a break or a vacation. Our minds never get a break or a vacation and seldom experience a moment's silence. Give your mind a break, a quiet place to go to clear, renew, and recharge.

Jenny, a client who was diagnosed with ovarian cancer, is an extreme example of what happens to a person's body and energy system when the mind and life become overloaded. In all of the years I have been reading for people, I had never experienced an interruption (such as someone at the door, phone problems, or electrical problems), until I spoke with Jenny, a high-powered executive who worked two jobs. Her work seemed to require her attention nearly twenty-four hours a day. She liked it that way. The feeling that she was always running out of time spurred her to make the most of it. She felt so fast, so speedy to me. I tried to speak to her about balance, some of the issues I have discussed in these pages, and others specifically pertinent to her. About twenty minutes into her one-hour reading, the phone went dead. I tried to call her back, but the line was busy. Finally, I received a call from her. Jenny explained that her electricity had gone out. As I continued talking to her about her high-voltage life and energy system, she began to interrupt, asking me to "hurry up and cut to the chase." This had never happened to me. Before I could get over my shock, the phone went dead again.

Jenny called back, saying that her regular phone had gone out and she was on her cell phone now. She assured me that no matter what universal force was trying to get in the way of our reading, she would not let that happen. I said I did not think it was interference from an outside force, but her own velocity that was setting off her home electrical systems and appliances. Again, the phone went dead. She called back from her second cell phone, and I continued the reading. Again, we were interrupted—this time by her burglar alarm.

Jenny never did seem to get the point I was trying to make about slowing down her fast-paced life, body, and energy through awareness and a meditation-relaxation process. I suggested many other things to her, but if the cancer that was robbing her of life could not get through to her, chances were small that she could hear anything or anyone else.

Jenny had trouble learning from her health lessons, but lessons are not wasted if they serve to help others. If your life is on fast-forward, like Jenny's, or you are an overthinker who cannot imagine what an empty mind might feel like even momentarily, consider a relaxation practice. There are many forms of meditation. It doesn't have to be formal, where you chant or need a guru. Meditation can be as simple as taking just a few moments, closing your eyes, and focusing on your breath. Whatever suits you is the right practice.

And *practice* is the operative word here. Relaxation is a skill that can be learned. Just as you learned how to be busy, you need to reach a level of fitness with relaxation. Take it easy and go slowly. Start with one minute a day, if necessary. In most client readings, no more than ten to twenty minutes per day is suggested. This is not a big time investment; however, this mental discipline delivers payoffs that can be enormous: increased ability to concentrate; quicker and more accurate decision making; fewer struggles with worry, guilt, and anger; and relief from insomnia are some of the benefits I have seen. The great Indian spiritual leader Paramahansa Yogananda says,

"Silence and seclusion are the secrets of success. In this modern life of activity, there is only one way to separate yourself from its ceaseless demands: get away from it once in a while."[8] Find that place inside yourself—it is always available to you.

My favorite meditation resource is an audiotape set by Jack Kornfield entitled *The Inner Art of Meditation*.[9] In this six-tape set encompassing his five-week course, he gently shows you how to meditate. Many people who have had trouble establishing a consistent practice, even those who have studied with numerous teachers and programs, find success with this audiotape set.

If a sitting meditation does not suit you, how about a moving one? Some people are just not meant to sit still and, in fact, experience negative feelings about it. If you are feeling negative about a practice, how much good will it do you? Little or none, I have found. If you are a kinesthetic person who really likes to move, consider walking meditation, tai chi, chi kung, or artistic expression. My friend who mountain bikes finds that it is his perfect expression of meditative practice. If he doesn't pay attention while biking on the edge of a cliff, if he worries about a future fall instead of being present, he does fall. If he is in the moment of now—focused, relaxed, and fear-free— he rides perfectly, in the flow, almost without thinking. Use whatever expression appeals to you and relaxes you. As long as you can commit to a moderate and consistent practice, it is the one for you.

Aside from all the physical, mental, emotional, and spiritual benefits, the most amazing thing about a meditation-relaxation practice is that it seems to expand time. People who take time from their busy day and invest in this practice seem to be less hurried and more relaxed, but somehow able to do more and do it well. They are balanced between "being" and "doing." Life seems easier, and it flows. My friend Lulu sometimes finds herself asking, "What's wrong with me? Why isn't anything going right today?" Then she realizes, "Oh. I didn't meditate." Remember to make time for yourself, to give your busy, hardworking mind the mental break it deserves.

DEPRESSION

When you cultivate a meditative practice, you are practicing a discipline—similar to a sport, hobby, or work ethic—and with this discipline comes awareness. You start to notice when your mind is dwelling or overfocusing on something unimportant, like an unneeded judgment, and how it can assume an all-consuming importance. A prime example of this is depression. Many people experience varying degrees of depression, from sadness to a lack of energy to an inability to do even the simplest things. Depression can be minor or incapacitating. My spiritual mentor, George, once told me, "Depression is a meditation on a transitory event or situation."

Think about that for a moment. See if it rings true. Many people resonate with this statement on an emotional, a mental, or a spiritual level. It may be easier to make this connection in the case of fleeting depression, that which lasts only a few hours, days, or weeks. When severe, long-lasting biochemical depression is present, it may be harder to pinpoint overfocusing as a component and to determine when or why it started.

There are many ways to move toward transcendence of depression—including forgiveness, self-love, working through fear—but first you must notice to what you are giving so much of your attention. If you have begun to cultivate the discipline of meditation through some sort of practice, you will be better equipped to take notice and to start to shift.

Depression can be a wall, and we may need more than just our own resources to climb over it. We sometimes need the help of a counselor and of alternative or conventional medicine. However, we can do our part by addressing these underlying levels; in partnership with the self, we can shift our focus from transitory events and situations and move into a healthier place.

SECTION II

CHAPTER 11

The Health Intuition Method

In section 1, I discussed the themes and issues that I perceive while conducting intuitive readings. In this section, I want to share with you how I actually do a reading. Section 1 ended on the subject of meditative practice. I find that the more that I incorporate practices that quiet the mind, the more easily I access my intuition. Not only does my intuitive ability seem smoother, but also the quality of impressions is more specific and accurate.

As part of my thesis research, I surveyed and interviewed many of my colleagues who are health/medical intuitives. How important was a meditative practice to them? A majority—89 percent—meditate. Some of the other activities I have mentioned to you as important for health and well-being were also cited as important to their intuitive ability. Seventy-eight percent cited creative expression and prayer, 67 percent mentioned exercise, and spiritual practice (anything that feels like a spiritual connection that is practiced with regularity) was included by all of them—100 percent. Not only are these practices beneficial in helping you shift and transcend old patterns and problems that keep you from your optimum health and well-being, they are also consistently practiced by professional intuitives and are considered important in enhancing intuitive ability.

WHAT IS HEALTH?

In chapter 7, I mentioned the Alex Grey workshop I attended. In addition to viewing the effect of meditation and divine connection on the human energy system, I got a very important message. During a visualization, I saw a gorgeous alexandrite. This jewel is usually grass-green; however, in certain light it can change to other colors. The explanation I intuitively heard was, "Everyone has their own version of health. Don't try to impose your vision of health on them." Like an ever-changing alexandrite, health means different things to different people. This vision can change with time for each person. The message of the alexandrite has taught me to deliver intuitive health information without being attached to the outcome. When I follow this guideline, I do not unduly influence or contaminate the client's attainment of his or her version of health.

Tuning in to Mitzi, a forty-four-year-old client, I received a reading that was primarily spiritual in content. As we spoke, the reading pointed her toward forgiveness, cleaning up old issues, coming to closure, and acknowledging and knowing her life purpose. Mitzi realized that the time had come to finish this part of her existence and move on. Her liver cancer was spreading like wildfire. She felt complete as we finished the reading. Mitzi knew what she needed to do. No advice was given on how to heal her body; rather, she was told to heal her spirit and soul and to begin the transition from this life to her next phase. She was satisfied.

When I shared her story with one of my students, Russell, he became very upset. I was illustrating how everyone holds a different vision of health and how that ideal can change throughout a lifetime. Russell could not understand why the reading did not give Mitzi the information she needed to cure her cancer and save her life. Russell's own existence was spent in pursuit of athletic endeavors. He feared and despised sickness and weakness. To Russell, health is a perfectly functioning body. To Mitzi, health (at this time in her life) centered around transition. She knew that her body was used up but her soul was everlasting. She put her concentration on the long-term investment—her soul—instead of the short-term investment, a quick fix that might give her a few extra days of pain and suffering in a cancer-ridden body. Health means different things to different people.

As you learn to intuit for yourself, remember these lessons I have learned and be gentle with yourself. I think learning to listen to yourself is the best gift you will ever give—or receive. What better act of self-nurturing? In chapter 13, I'll describe a simple three-step process you can use to intuit. I'll teach you how to tune in and listen to yourself, to find the meaning behind your own "check engine" lights, your own levels of health and well-being and how to improve them.

CHAPTER 12

Before You Tune In . . .

Intuitive information can be a wonderful adjunct to "check engine" lights and facts we already know. I may be aware that my ear hurts, but I want to know the mental, emotional, or spiritual components that contribute to this condition. Author Milton Fisher quotes this amazing statistic in one of his books: "It has been estimated that between 60 and 75 percent of all medical problems are causes aggravated by anxiety, fear, pain and depression. . . . The term *psychosomatic* describes real diseases whose genesis is in the mind."[1]

If we can use our intuition to identify the components behind our psychosomatic imbalances and to learn what to do about them, we can work to clear up our problems more quickly.

YOUR NEW FRIEND

When you first try to tune in, you may have trouble getting answers. You might think that your intuition is not working, and that may be the case. Did you come out of the womb knowing how to walk? Probably not. Although I believe everyone possesses intuitive ability to some degree, it may be lying dormant. You might need to wake it up. How do you do that? Just as you awaken a person: You knock on the door, you speak to him or her, you gently shake them—in short, you keep at it until something works.

Perhaps your intuition will speak so softly to you that you will have trouble hearing it. Think of intuition as a new, shy friend. When you meet someone and there is a connection, you may try to pursue that potential friendship. Slowly, you get to know each other, and each of you decides whether this is a good fit. You cultivate the relationship in stages—it is very unlikely that you would develop a solid, best-friend relationship overnight. Intuition needs to be cultivated too. Give it attention, as you would to a new friend. Listen; don't do all the talking. Gradually, your new friend, which is really your own inner guidance, will become more confident about sharing with you.

Some people's intuition is more like a pushy acquaintance. Do you recall meeting someone like this? The two of you made a connection and were excited about a future friendship. The person calls, then calls again, then keeps asking you to do something—a little too fast for your comfort level. What do you do? You set boundaries. You say, "No, not today." Or "This is moving a little too quickly for me. Would you mind slowing down?" If the potential friend listens, great. If not, you might say something like, "This is not a good fit for me. Good-bye." Time passes, and you find a friendship that does work for you, on your terms.

You are in charge of your intuition. One of my favorite quotes, from Matthew 7:7, is, "Ask and it will be given to you; seek and you will find; knock and the door will be opened." These are such beautiful, simple, and direct words. Look for and listen to that guidance within yourself, and connect to that higher source; both are the well-spring of intuition.

I believe anyone can be intuitive. In fact, I'm convinced that everyone *is*. Like any other sense, intuition can be enhanced through intention and practice. Most of us are familiar with the idea that if someone becomes blind, their other senses become stronger to help compensate. They may hear incredibly well or be able to recognize individuals just by their scent—information that many of us are unaware of. The same holds true with intuition: if you concentrate on receiving information intuitively, your ability to do so will get better and better.

Some people are afraid: "What if it gets *too* good? What if I pick up information that I find upsetting?" These are valid concerns.

Intuition also needs boundaries. When you are driving your car, it may be permissible for you to receive an impression at a stoplight, as long as it is quick and not so upsetting that you are unable to drive when the light turns green. It would be unacceptable to drive down the street and receive psychic insights about the traumas and problems of the people inside every house you pass. First, it would be too distracting; second, what would be the purpose? It's not as if you can go up to the door and give the residents your irrelevant (or relevant) intuitive impressions. It would be impossible, inappropriate, and unwelcome. Set your boundaries with your intuition, just as you would with a friend. If intuition doesn't work for you one way, decide what will and ask for your intuitive impressions to come in that format.

I cannot watch horror movies. Sometimes even a scary episode of a television show will make me cover my eyes and ask whoever is in the room to tell me what's happening. If it is too frightening, I turn the TV off. Thus, although I am able to use my intuition in many areas, I choose not to become involved in police work. It is a wonderful service, and I am grateful for the people who do this important work. However, I know that my lack of comfort with frightening situations would get in the way of my impressions or bother me so much that I could not live a healthy life. I set my intuitive boundaries so that I do not receive "scary" information. This does not mean that I have shut off a part of myself so that my clients cannot be helped. Instead of seeing a visual image of someone being horribly abused as a child, for example, I will hear the phrase *horribly abused as a child*. I still receive information; I just get it in a format that does not incapacitate me with fright. Set your boundaries. I use an invocation (see chapter 13) to help set my intuitive boundaries.

MULTIPLE CHANNELS

Using more than one intuitive frequency can be of great help. I am primarily a visual intuitive—that's how my first impressions started. Secondarily, I hear information, so I am not only *clairvoyant* (from the French for "clear seeing"), but *clairaudient* ("clear hearing") as well. And early in my experience as a health intuitive, I discovered that I have a third way of sensing: through my body, which is known as *clairsentience* ("clear sensing") or *kinesthetic*.

I had conducted all of my readings in person until I evaluated Ling, a forty-four-year-old woman who lived thousands of miles away from me on the East Coast of the United States. As I was conducting the reading, I did not understand what I saw. I said to her: "I see your left knee, but I feel it in my right knee. [Before the reading I had no knee pain, but this pain felt so real, so intense, that I had to mention it.] I'm confused and don't know how to resolve this."

"There's no conflict," Ling said. "Both of my knees are shot." It was hard for me to tell Ling that I did not understand what I was seeing or feeling. I wanted to appear confident and knowledgeable. But, by sharing my quandary with her, I learned the meaning of what I was seeing and sensing and—more important—I learned a valuable lesson. I believe that a reading can't be a "hit"—an accurate interpretation—if you don't share the information. If I had kept my impressions to myself, I would never have had the feedback that her right knee was bad too. It takes courage to be intuitive, especially when the impressions are unusual, do not make sense, or seem foolish.

Before Ling's reading, I hadn't "felt" a client's symptoms in my body. Of course, in everyday life, I'd felt chills up and down my spine or butterflies in my stomach. These gut reactions mostly concerned safety issues. I never thought of them as intuitive, but now I realize they were. You may notice a certain feeling that comes over you when people lie to you or are about to share joyful news with you. Katrina is an editor with a major book publisher. She said: "A certain feeling wells up inside me when I need to ask a question, but I'm not sure whether it's a good idea. The same feeling comes up when I need to assert myself in an uncomfortable situation. From experience, I know that if I think of asking a question when I'm unsure of myself, but I have this feeling, I should ask—I get positive results. If I don't get the feeling yet ask, I usually end up looking foolish. The same holds true for the assertiveness piece." Paying attention to feelings and their results will help you to live a life more intuitively, with better flow. And it's an easy way to practice your intuition.

After my experience with Ling, when I felt pain or other sensations in my body during a reading, I was disturbed and a little frightened that I was receiving information this way. I called an intuitive friend and told her about my anxiety. Her warm answer put my mind at ease: "Honey, it doesn't matter what channel you get the information on, as long as you get the right stuff!"

I've gotten to the point where I realize the value in having more than one channel to verify information and use as a double check. A few years ago, I went mushroom hunting in the mountains. I rode up with a friend who wanted to mountain bike while I was hiking. Raul and I agreed to meet in two hours. Four hours later he came out of the mountains, holding his hand above his head. He seemed to be in shock. He had fallen, hard, and landed on his hand. As I piled him into the car to take him to the emergency room, he asked, "Is it broken?" I tuned in.

Visually, I saw his little finger in two pieces, one piece slightly on top of the other. But the voice inside my head said, "Not broken, no permanent damage." Conflicting information, it would seem. I was too busy driving down the mountain to intuit further. When we arrived at the hospital, the contradiction was resolved. The X-ray showed the finger in two pieces, one on top of the other, but it was dislocated, not broken. If I had gone with my visual image, which was correct, but had *interpreted* it with my limited medical knowledge as broken, I would have been wrong. My interpretation would have been a "miss," even though my impression was correct.

Later in this book, I will teach you the value of open-ended questions and how asking better questions leads to better answers. A yes-no question (such as, "Is it broken?") leaves too many possibilities uncovered. It gives you so little information. Usually, if clients ask one, I ask them to restate their question as an open-ended query (who, what, when, where, why, and how, for example). Be careful what you assume. If you are unsure, ask follow-up questions. (With Raul, I was in a rush and concerned, so I tuned in almost immediately.)

Getting the "right stuff" is important, but I find my "misses" are some of the best teachers. Henry Ford believed the same thing:

> Intuitive reactions, I find, are usually valuable even if they prove to be wrong. They give me an instant basis with which to compare alternatives that may later be developed in the more usual ways of corporate practice. And when my intuition's right in the first instance, I am that far ahead at the outset.[2]

INTUITIVE VOCABULARY

Interpreting what you see, hear, and feel not only takes courage, it takes practice. About a year after I began doing readings, I was privately tutored in anatomy by a physician who taught the course in medical school. This gave me the language with which to communicate to others in the health care field. Instead of saying something like, "It's that thing that looks like a sewer pipe that runs down the throat toward the belly," I could say *esophagus*, saving the health care professional confusion and time.

As I have become more experienced, I have also learned symbology. To me, symbols are the universal language. I've heard people say that mathematics is the only universal language, but what is math other than symbols with meanings? You can find symbols the world over. A symbol may mean the same thing to many different cultures. As I have grown as an intuitive, my symbolic vocabulary has grown too. This saves me time; I think of symbols as a shortcut. I now have set symbols for certain things such as illnesses, events, emotions, and behaviors. For example, I see diabetes as a pancreas that looks like the desert after a rainstorm—like mud that dries quickly and leaves a cracked surface. I did not always know this. It took practice. The first time I got this impression, I shared it with the client, who told me he had diabetes. The second time I saw the desert-pancreas symbol, the client also had diabetes. Eventually I realized that this was my symbol for diabetes. The symbology I have developed not only covers physical problems a client may have, it covers situations too. I have symbols for rape, abuse, artistry, prayer life, and many other situations.

Years ago, I was having breakfast with Caroline Myss and two of her friends, Arthur and Tabitha. While Arthur was talking, I kept getting the feeling that he had prostate cancer. Since I had just met him, and I had very little experience with intuitive impressions, I said nothing. Ten minutes later, Arthur said to us, "I have prostate cancer." I could barely eat or speak for the rest of the meal. As we were leaving, I privately shared with Caroline what I had experienced. She said, "Remember the quality of that impression. The quality is always the same." Her words taught me to look for the unique visuals, audios, or feelings in each impression, so that I could use them to develop my symbolic intuitive vocabulary.

Here is an example of symbology from the introductory paragraph of a reading:

Reading on Sabra, age twenty-nine

Sabra, you beautiful girl, woman, child, soul, being. You are many things to many people, including yourself. Instead of seeing this as a problem, wishing you were more a synthesis of one, think of how fortunate it is. It's like you can jump into any suit/role/character/being— meaning you—and be perfect for the situation. [*I explained to her that I saw her in a bat suit, with the bat-cycle, like Catwoman, but there was no mask! It was as if she* was *her, not portraying a character.*] No mask is important to you; these are all genuine aspects of you. You are integrated, even if you feel dysfunctional and disjointed. Change your view and perspective and you will begin to feel more comfortable with who you are and the many different and wonderful aspects that make up beautiful Sabra. [*Here I described to her the image I had symbolizing her. She was in the hub or center of a wheel. There were spokes going out from the center, and she was able to move along each spoke and be something different for each situation or person. She was not playacting; she was really herself.*] Listen to your own voice, not that of others, as you follow your heart and mind in congru-ence to where your will feels manifest and loved. You know, deep inside; you don't need others to tell you.

Pause for a moment here. Do you know what I was describing to my client? Focus specifically on the hub/wheel analogy. Another clue: no masks, but really her. Stop and think—what is this symbolizing to the client? One last clue: "Listen to your own voice, not that of oth-ers." Sabra heard my introduction and shakily said, "Do you know what you are describing?"

"You mean a diagnosis? No," I replied.

"I have multiple personality disorder," she said.

Our reading was an incredible time of learning for me, and of beauty as well. I was able to see the creativity with which she had developed these personalities in response to horrible abuse. She did not develop a mental illness that keeps her from fulfilling her duties, but one in which she was able to function on many levels as many aspects of her whole. Mental illness has always been a little unsettling to me, possibly because I have little or no experience with it other than what I see on television, where it is usually portrayed in a frightening light. That day, I got to see someone working with her burdens and traumas while functioning in a way that made her life possible. I thank Sabra and all my clients for helping me understand the symbology of what I see.

Every intuitive is different. What symbolizes dry pancreas for me will mean nothing to you. It's like when you read the meaning of a symbol in a dream dictionary, and you think, *This makes no sense!* We need six billion dream dictionaries, a different one for each person on our planet, because we each have our own dialect of intuitive symbology. If you've ever tried to learn a foreign language, you know how much practice and patience it takes. You are learning your own foreign language: symbology. It takes time, but once you know the symbols, you will know the meaning. And, just like learning anything, there are always new things to discover—my symbolic vocabulary is still growing, daily.

TURNING OFF A CHANNEL

Because every intuitive is different, we all have different levels of comfort. Again, setting boundaries about how you take in information is important. I shut off my kinesthetic sense when I am doing readings. I customized my invocation to do so. I ask that I not take anything into my body. It is very uncomfortable for me to feel the pain or disease of another person in my body. Also, I believe it distracts me from the reading. So, with my two other channels (visual and audio) on, I leave the kinesthetic off. Just because I have shut mine off does not mean you need to as well. Most people have a kinesthetic channel. Every one of the medical intuitives I interviewed for my master's thesis uses the kinesthetic channel. Many health care workers I have talked to have "radar" fingers and hands—they intuitively know where a patient hurts.

If you find that one of the channels bothers you, as long as you have two others open for double checking, customize your invocation (I will teach you how to do an invocation in chapter 13, "Tuning In") and ask for that channel to be turned off for the reading. For example, I say, "I ask that my kinesthetic channel be turned off."

If you decide you want to turn one of your channels off, you need to remember to do so each time you tune in to do a reading. I have never had a problem reading for someone as long as I remember to do my invocation, but if I forget to protect myself, I can get into trouble. Recently, I was reading a man from Canada. As with every reading, I tune in before our session, so that I have the information at hand. When I tuned in to him, I felt overwhelmed with darkness, tiredness, and heaviness, as if I could not move. I called him and asked if we could do the reading another day. He agreed. For two days, I felt this way. I finally figured it out: I had forgotten to invoke "I ask that I not take this into my body" when I began his reading. He was nearly crippled with depression and fatigue, as was I from taking his energy into my body. Once I realized this, and freed myself of his energy, I was able to do the reading accurately and with no adverse effect on myself.

MY STYLE

Accuracy is important, so I was initially very troubled when it became apparent that I do not intuitively receive a lot of disease names when I read for clients. At first I thought this meant I was not doing a good job. I reasoned that if I were an accurate intuitive, I would receive disease names. But not receiving them has turned out for the best.

Clients often say something like, "You described my symptoms perfectly. Do you know what disease the doctors say this is?" I usually have to say no. Then they tell me that they have been diagnosed with a certain disease. Clients, without exception, seem to prefer that I am not labeling them. They like the fact that I get the symptoms, what is behind them, how they work together as a group, and what can be done about them, but that I do not put them into a category. As time goes on, my intellectual side remembers when a certain manifestation of symptoms equals a disease that I have seen before, but by and large, my intuitive side still gets symptoms, not disease labels.

Even without disease labels, my clients still get the message. About a year ago, I read for a client and asked her to get her breasts checked, as I saw "great potential for breast unhealth." I did not use the word *cancer* with her because I intuitively felt this would scare her. Although I did not say *cancer,* my wording was still specific enough to be of use. (I feel it is irresponsible to "suggest" a future disease to someone when it has not manifested. The mind is powerful, and I have seen it create disease. I also feel it is a disservice to be vague.) She immediately went for a breast check. Nothing showed up on the mammogram, but her doctor noticed a skin irregularity and took a small sample of surrounding tissue. It was analyzed and found to contain microscopic cancer cells, about two millimeters in width. My client's doctor feels that if she had not come in and insisted on a thorough breast check, this cancer would have been found in a much later stage. My client credits her reading with saving her life. I credit the whole team—medical practitioner, intuitive, and client/patient— for discovering the cancer and working toward recovery.

CASE STUDIES

To give you an idea of one of my readings, here is an excerpt from an actual evaluation. Not only did the client give feedback, but her physician was present as well, verifying her disease and creating a treatment plan based on the information the three of us had gathered. I have bracketed and italicized summaries of the feedback from the client and her doctor. I have left these readings in their actual form: the grammar is incorrect and the language switches from first person to third person. This will give you an idea of the actual flavor of an evaluation and not set up false expectations that your own readings will be grammatically perfect.

Reading on Lisa, age fifty-six

Lisa, you have requested a health and life purpose reading. I will give you the life purpose information first, followed by the health. Both are important, for if one is aligned with their life purpose, one's health is thereby more vibrant; on the other hand, if one's health is optimum, one is more easily able to achieve their life purpose, so it is a yin/yang kind of effect.

Life Purpose

Lisa, all of your life you have been waiting for something; it's almost a hunger inside you. You want to be a part of something, but you've had trouble figuring out what it is. You like to join things—organizations, clubs, others—but haven't found it to be quite the fulfilling thing you are looking for. Perhaps it's because that fulfilling thing is deep inside you, and you need to bring it from the inside out in order to manifest what you're looking for and to teach others.

Teaching is what it is all about for you. Ever since you were a little girl, you have loved and longed to teach others. I keep getting a vision of you sharing, being generous, even to the sharing of flowers, it looks like. Does gardening hold a special interest for you? It seems like that would be a wonderful way for you to express your creativity. [*Lisa and her physician, Dr. Still, laughed. Her home was filled with flowers and plants, and she actually took care of Dr. Still's when he was out of town. She was also trained as a florist.*] I actually get that the master gardener's program would be excellent for you, if you have not already taken it. Then, you could fulfill another need—in addition to teaching—which is volunteering and making a difference; showing others how to grow their own food, flowers, gardens—information that has long ceased to be handed down from generation to generation.

It's almost as if a club or organization has to informally form around you. I keep getting a vision of an old, wooden, beautiful spoke wheel, and you at the center of this with your arms outstretched, giving, sharing, showing your love in this way.

This vision of flowers even extends to where I see you in a flowery hat and a flower-print dress, surrounding yourself with flowers, and their aroma is very important to you. I would even suggest in the winter months—when they are not so plentiful—surrounding yourself with aromatherapy in the bath would be a lovely thing for you and aid in peacefulness and relaxation.

What I keep getting over and over is that you long to be a part of the earth, its nourishment and giving to others. It's almost as if you are an extension of the earth mother, and by doing things with and for the earth, you can most easily manifest your life purpose. It's not so much a path of service to others, but to yourself, a path of service to the earth.

Be careful, though, not to get caught up in too many environmental causes, as they will zap the energy right out of your body. You can pick one or two, but be careful not to get overly caught up or overwrought in them, as you really take things about the earth, and her little animals, to heart. [*Lisa confirmed that it was hard on her metaphorical heart to see plants and animals not treated well.*]

You are such a kind and caring person. It really seems that your life purpose is to spread this love and kindness like fertilizer on the plants and those who want to learn these ways from you. I definitely see you starting a loose-knit organization where you are teaching people how to grow their own food, etc. Be careful that you don't get too caught up in the administration/paperwork side of this, as you are pretty good at that, but that's not your purpose. You can always get someone else to do that; your task is to teach, to share, to get your hands in the earth. I see you surrounded by children of all colors, showing them the beauty of a plant growing, and hearing their *oohs* and *aahs* in return. You may not even be doing this in your town; this actually appears to be a poorer neighborhood—or inner-city youth—that you would reach. I actually know of someone who has done something somewhat like this for many years, and if this interests you, and you want to get in touch, I will give you their number.

FINAL LIFE PURPOSE MESSAGE:

Blessings to you, blessings of the earth to you and others. Your blessing of life purpose will be a blessing of the soil, of the knowledge of the fruits of the soil given to others. It's a very earthy life purpose that awaits you. Manifest it if you can, as it will be more fruitful than you ever dreamed possible.

Health

Lisa's health is unpredictable. One minute up, one minute down. I see an image of her huffing and puffing and wiping her brow. What does this image bring up for her? I get a yes on tiredness, but it also seems like she is somewhat out of shape, and perhaps over-weight. [*Lisa was about 50 pounds overweight.*] It's a catch-22, as she seems maybe too tired to exercise. Did she once have a weight or eating disorder? [*Both.*] This factors in. Her body is off balance because it doesn't know what to do with nutrition. This is a big deal with her. It's like her body has been given so many mixed messages with food that it doesn't know what to do, how to process even the good stuff. More greens would be of help in getting this back in bal-ance—somewhat of a mineral deficiency, but definitely more of a vitamin deficiency. Pills don't seem easily absorbed. Can she take vitamins in liquid form? Colloidal is one possibility, but actually, an IV push here might be of great help. [*I did not know what an IV push is, as my intuition often gets terms that I do not know or understand. Lisa's physician did know what an IV push is and agreed he would look into it as a likely idea.*] I get a big yes on this. Just a boost to get her back in balance. I get a yes on acupuncture, but more of a positive yes on acupressure. When I picture her with needles, I get a fearful stance—what does this bring up for you? [*Lisa said she was horribly afraid of needles.*] That's why the touching arts seem to be a better fit: acupressure, acu-yoga, acu-diet. This is strange. That word *acu-diet* is defined for me as "acupressure while eating to aid digestion." Dr. Still, what do you think of this? Can this be accomplished? [*Dr. Still is a physician who also practices acupuncture. He was excited about the possibility and agreed to look into it.*]

Although nutrition is certainly the base for problems, there are other issues too. Let's start at the bottom of the body and work our way up:

Feet: There really appears to be a problem here with one foot, and I am having difficulty discerning which foot. [*Lisa said her right foot is worse, but both feet are not so good.*] Perhaps that's because it is both. Specifically, I keep getting an image of some foot deformity, like women get from wearing shoes that aren't right for their feet, or potentially some vascular circulation problems due to a goutlike condition. [*Lisa said she had to wear very supportive shoes now, like Birkenstocks, and that she has gout.*] This makes sense due to the nutritional problems. I get that alfalfa would help here. Also, some massage or rolfing, if she wants to commit to that. It feels like there is also stiffness in the ankles, but perhaps I am misinterpreting this image—I see someone trying to rotate her feet around and around at the ankles, and them not being very open to this [*confirmed by both Lisa and her doctor*].

Emotionally, I get that Lisa was abused as a child by a close family member, perhaps a brother, a male for sure. This also took the form of merciless teasing, which was very hard on her. It was a struggle, as it seems like this is not abuse by cultural definition, but her very perception of it, and the constant nature of it, really made it abusive. [*Lisa's real name is somewhat masculine. She did suffer abuse from her father and brother, and was teased constantly about her name.*] She is such a loving person that it was hard to understand. The father seems closed off to me; I get an image of his arms across his chest—what does this bring up for you? [*Lisa said that her father was like that the last time she saw him, in his casket. He was incredibly closed off to her while alive.*] To me, it's almost like he wouldn't interfere on your behalf. Not so much physically as emotionally cold. In order for the feet and legs to have improved health, one of the shifts she can make is to go back and forgive those instances, whenever they come up, each situation, ask for help and she'll get it, to let it go. The purpose of this abuse was in giving her a thicker skin, which she would need in the business and/or family world. Because she is so loving, it's almost like she had to be overexposed in order to develop this skin. This is also why I think the extra weight is there, more like padding. The image I received of her was like she was in a suit, like the Stay Puff Marshmallow Man, and she was ready to burst forth, unzipping the suit, and emerging, like Wonder Woman! [*Lisa liked this image.*]

Legs seem bloated; is there water retention going on here? Again, more of this padding. It doesn't feel like there is good circulation throughout the lower extremities. Again, it's almost as if she is willing the "blood" to circulate, as blood family was hard for her to deal with. Perhaps a more positive picture is to replace it with her current family or friends in her image and let the "new blood family flow freely." Almost seems as if the gait is stilted, again, same thing—family of origin. [*Confirmed.*]

Knees feel creaky, again same thing. One hip is lower than the other. I get an image of her carrying a child on one hip. What does this bring up for you? Youngster caring for the younger? It feels like a hardworking childhood. [*This was confirmed by both Lisa and her doctor.*] Female organs, seems like she is mostly past menopause, as it is dormant in there. Another good reason to creatively express her energy, to keep that center alive and flowing with the crone; instead of needing to be the fertility goddess with her womb, she can be her through her gardening expression.

Interesting image here: I keep getting an image of a cord tightly wrapping around and around her waist, constricting it—what image does this bring up for you? [*Trouble with getting enough breath and also wanting to lose weight.*]

Liver appears to be enlarged—toxicity from bingeing and purging. Maybe not even with food, but with life threats—what does this mean to her? [*She feels threatened all of the time. Can't even make friends aside from her husband. She is always feeling sick from the threat of everyday living. She takes it all in, and then blows up, like a volcano—very stressful.*]

Kidneys seem to be a little dark, not too vibrant. Again, the waterways really seem like they aren't circulating well. Family stuff, as we discussed before.

There seems to be a lot of stuff going on with the third chakra organs, area of the solar plexus; also, spleen looks enlarged, and not from a Chinese medicine point of view. Pancreas looks crusty like mud after a big rain and dried in the sun. Diabetes? [*The physician and she had suspected this.*] The impression I get is that although you are now in a loving and positive relationship, it wasn't always so. And you draw a great deal of energy and strength from others' opinions of you. Despite your thick skin, you are sometimes just getting an "arrow to the gut" that strikes into these organs and really hurts you. You take things very personally, because you are so caring of a person. What to do, what to do? Well, what you can do is stop smoking. [*It wasn't smoking, it was her work. She inhaled a lot of carbon monoxide at her job, which she hated, running an automotive repair shop.*] Give up addictions and crutches. Another thing you can do is to find your own spiritual side, and not rely on organized religion to give you everything in terms of a divine spiritual life and connection. Actually, if you fill yourself up with divine presence, you will find yourself less and less likely to think of what others are thinking of you, and when they try to zing you, the arrow will bounce off harmlessly. It's not an even thicker skin you need, it's an internal radiance, like a force field, that will protect and start to heal you. Nice image!

Heart area: I really get you heaving for breath—what is going on here? I actually get that you have trouble taking in breath due to altitude? It's almost as if the chemical reaction between water and oxygen in your body that needs to happen can't because your water is so bound up in your tissues—skin tissues, especially. It's not circulating, either. If I had to pick one word for problems in you, it's *circulation*. [*Again, seems to be the auto repair shop environment where she works.*] When I ask what you can do to change this, I get an image of you unzipping and stepping out of your current body, like it was a padded suit you wore over your new body, breaking free of the bonds of the old body. You can do this by lightly stepping up your exercise, but more important, focusing on the inner you, the one that is bursting, dying to come out. This inner you is a loving person who can take and receive love and nourishment from those around her, including her nutritional need for food. She can love and be loved, nourish and be nourished, and there is an even exchange going on in her life, instead of her always giving and being afraid to take. You have a lovely, peaceful, blue energy about you, and you won't lose this, but you will be more active and dynamic in your energy.

Neck pain around C7, behind the will chakra center. [*Confirmed by physician.*] I get a coughing motion too. The will seems to be supplanted (interesting choice of words) by letting others control and choose for you, instead of you manifesting what you want. Yes, it can be easier, in the short run, but in the long run, it just leaves you feeling resigned, see big sigh. [*Confirmed.*]

Clicking jaw. Funky teeth—dentures? [*No to dentures, yes to jaw.*] I get a big image of you swallowing your words—what is this? And them grating as they go down your throat, scraping your esophagus, and lying in your belly, very hard to digest. This is another part of the digestion puzzle. Next time you eat your words, remember that doesn't leave room for the nourishment and food you need in your belly!

Nose: see sneezing, allergies? Hay fever can be helped through elimination of certain food allergens in your diet. Would she be willing to go on some sort of an allergy-reduction diet? Wheat doesn't feel too bad, corn is big, dairy is huge, would be my guess. Citrus is a little too acidic for her at this point in life. Some kind of sinus problems, at least. [*Correct.*]

When I look at your intellectual and intuition center, they are a big, bright purple/lavender flower. Lovely! You are so smart, and actually very intuitive, although you like to shut that out, because since you already know a lot about people through your intelligence, you don't know what you'd do with all that extra information that might create more problems. Oooh! But sometimes, you let the intuition flow. It's kind of a start/stop pinwheel action. It seems like you need to get in the flow all the time and learn not to be afraid of it. *Psychic Pathway*[3] would be an excellent book for you.

Your hair seems kind of thin to me—and dry skin

too. [*Yes.*] Okay, here's the scoop: Your relationship with the divine is not very one-on-one; it's very organization-related. I see you in church clapping your hands and singing and enjoying yourself. [*Lisa laughed long and hard. I used the expression holy roller to describe what I was seeing. A term I learned growing up, and I mean it in the most positive way: It's someone who really gets into gospel music and moves, sings, and dances along. She said she was so attracted to gospel music that in the past week she had bought several compact discs.*] In reality, though, it seems like you don't have to stop enjoying that. You can still go, but you need to do individual prayer, meditation, whatever, all the time throughout the day. Let it be a natural part of your life. Accessing your intuition is a natural part of opening this up too; these two areas can help each other. Then this divine energy connection can just flow down into your body and give you the power to make the changes you want.

Other things I might have missed: feels like back pain behind kidneys, feels like hands are stiff and in pain, see her rubbing them. Back stuff relates to kidney/plexus, as we discussed earlier. Hands I see being helped by working more in the earth, changing diet, eating more greens. [*Accurate.*]

FINAL MESSAGE:

Lisa, you are a beautiful and worthwhile soul who is perched on a pinnacle of transformation for yourself. I get an image of you standing at a crossroads, not knowing which way to go. [*Although her marriage was generally solid, she was on shaky ground when it came to learning to set boundaries with her husband. He liked to tell her what to do. After decades of marriage, she was starting to say no.*] You have been given some suggestions about things you can choose, ways you can go, what you can look toward, but in the end, it is up to you, and your intuition, to choose and decide what's right for you. No one else can, or should, make these decisions for you. And making these decisions will leave you feeling self-satisfied. [*Image of her smiling, hands on her hips, proudly and happily surveying her garden and the garden of life.*]

Lisa and Dr. Still declared the reading to be 98 percent accurate. Remember, I use only a client's name and age to tune in; the rest of the information comes intuitively.

Now that you have seen an example of a reading, you might be thinking, *I could never do that.* You're right. You can't. Your readings will not be exactly like mine. Each intuitive is different, and each client is an individual. Therefore, each person's reading will be specific to him or her. By reading my evaluation of Lisa, you can see what my format is for one person's reading—another person's will be totally different. Certainly, there are similarities throughout the readings I do: I concentrate on elements that are important to me—kindness, practicality, and compassion, for example. I mold my reading technique to suit the client. After all, the reading is for the client, not me. One client may want guidance about treatment modalities or practitioners, another may have the emotional or financial resources to deal with only a few issues, and yet another may be ready to dig deeply into pain and trauma.

Lisa's reading happened early in my career. The following is an excerpt from another reading, with a different flavor, conducted later in my career. You can see how my style has evolved, but also how each client's reading is different. When I was writing this book, I called my clients to see if I could include them and their readings (I practice strict confidentiality and have changed names and other identifying information). At that time, I asked Amanita for more feedback on the accuracy of the reading. Some of her comments are included in the bracketed notes in this excerpted reading.

Reading on Amanita, age thirty-nine

Amanita, you beautiful, beautiful being, much have you suffered, looking everywhere for answers and an end to your suffering. Let's look and see if we can give you some insights into this terrible ordeal and some requirements for positive shift and changes. [*She's been ill since 1991, diagnosed in 1998.*]

Feet: I see you moving them very gingerly; Amanita's feet are telling her, "Be careful where you move, walk, stop, care. Be careful where you go or look, for if you are not careful, you could be hurt." This stems from age seventeen; Amanita was betrayed by her father. [*Amanita says he was explosive and controlling. She had been away from home for a year and came back to live there at seventeen. This time frame really resonates for her. She felt like she was trapped, like there was no way out. She also realized that she was unable to get unconditional love as a child or as an adult. This time cemented for her the pattern of tiptoeing around, so as to avoid upsetting others. She said this time at home showed her she didn't matter, and it was all about "doing the dance"—making herself for other people, instead of being her real self. Amanita's dad was having an affair with her mom's friend. Amanita felt betrayed because there was no*] *trust or support for her. This pattern carried on to her adult life as a desire to be perfect.*] Her reasoning is that if you are perfect, there is no reason for someone to try to hurt you. Amanita's inability to look, based on this past trauma, is what keeps her from seeing clearly, fully, completely. She can't see the "whole truth and nothing but the truth" because she is afraid. How to shift this? Psychotherapy, hypnotic regression, with a competent, certified therapist, need to release this wound completely before going on. Someone who has body-mind therapy background. [*Eight months later, she is working with a body-mind therapist.*]

Almost a grayness to the lower leg area, something I have seen in the past in MS patients, but different. This is not MS, but it feels like there is a gradual shutting down of the nerve area, nerve pathways; messages can no longer travel at the speed they once did—have you noticed a tendency to shuffle? Image of shuffle, shoulders down, head down. [*Amanita states she been diagnosed with Lyme disease. According to her, it is often misdiagnosed as MS. It is a neurological disease. She has nerve weakness in legs.*]

Amanita has no self-esteem; she feels like loving herself would be a sin, would be incomprehensible. [*Eight months later, after psychotherapy, she is able to hear the negative self-talk she sends to herself, i.e., "You're so stupid." At the initial time of the reading, she was not conscious of this behavior, but now realizes it was always present.*]

How to shift this? Amanita, you are a loving person; you can see that you love others. How would you feel if they rejected it at every turn? That's how you feel, how your body feels. You need to think about that to help you open up to receive your own love and loving. If you can't love yourself first, last, best, and always, who will? [*Eight months later, working on this in psychotherapy, she is learning to forgive the "Why can't I be perfect?" imprinted by her father, family situation, and her own choices. She has carried this perfection pattern into her adulthood. She feels that trying harder, all the time, for so long has tired her out.*] It's the ultimate self-responsibility, and one that you shirk from (see shirking/cringing almost away). The reason you do this is that if you become strong, you are worried that it will be easier for those to knock you down. [*Amanita is very considerate of others. She wants people to like her. This is very important and she made herself who she needed to be in order for this to happen. I told her her reasoning was that, "If people like me, they won't hurt me." She agreed.*] It's almost as if you want to be invisible, don't want to be seen. Again, deep psychotherapy, as these are big, deep wounds. Need to start there before any other kind of therapy is effective.

Hips, butt: see your hands back of butt moving hips a little side to side—almost a weight shift? What is this? [*Pain in hips, knees, and joints.*]

Amanita wants to have a baby, but can't seem to manifest. [*She lost a baby in 1992 and wants to have one.*] Amanita, until you learn to love yourself fully and completely—take that self-responsibility of love to you first—things like that can't seem to happen for you. It's about reclaiming your own babyhood, childhood, teenager-hood, young adulthood, and most important, the self. [*She says this makes all the sense in the world.*]

Start with painting too; start to express without self-criticism; release the voices in the head through self-forgiveness, quiet time, alone, in a sunny spot, creating, very therapeutic, art therapy, if you'd like to call it that. [*Eight months later, she says she felt creatively "dead" at the time of the reading. Not enough energy to pursue. Since the reading, she has made some time and tried painting, which led to pottery. She finds this a real lesson in not becoming attached, as some of her art has blown up in the kiln. Her pottery is a metaphor for many things in her life.*]

Back: lower back, hand there, pain, crying. [*Severe, not constant, low back, sacrum.*] Amanita is worried about money and worries about other things—nonstop worrier. [*Yes. Not nitpicky, more of a "what if . . .?"*] *Energy of Money* a great tape to address these two areas. Feels like she might have been in some kind of human traction trying to straighten this out? [*Low back put into traction by chiropractor.*] Needs a more gentle craniosacral approach. Will help female area to release and unblock, along with art therapy. [*Eight months later, she feels this is helping her maintain, if not improve.*]

Pancreas: dry, wilting—how's your blood sugar? [*Tests are fine, but feels like it is stressed. She says Lyme can affect blood sugar.*] It's that issue of responsibility to self. This is one of the few things you've ever done for yourself (this reading), entirely for you—more of that energy, that idea, behind your motivations. Who am I doing this for? Me? Should I feel guilty, no? What if I do, so what? That's the kind of place to cultivate and be. Watch carbohydrates, need to lower the quick ones to help here [*she says carbos affect her blood sugar*], shots to help this. [*She has an allergy to nightshades; potatoes might be a possibility.*]

Liver: looks like it's ready to explode with fear; get in with a Chinese medical doctor right away to balance liver/kidney, lung/skin, organs. [*Acupuncturist says liver/kidney main focal point, along with spleen/pancreas. Her Western medical doctor says that her liver has been affected by prescription drugs.*] Liver warehouse holds on all the fear, kidneys the unspoken anger at the father and the self and all men; age twenty-two? [*This is right after a "honeymoon" period with her new boyfriend. She says things got "sticky," and she felt, "Wait a minute, I'm important. What I want to do is important too." She is still working through this, as she married this man.*]

Lungs: covering the heart, trying to avoid trouble, heartache being seen. You are trying to make yourself scarce (and scared is where you live); therefore scarcity of breath ensues. [*Shallow breath, needs to learn how to take in a complete breath.*]

And skin: see itching? Really feels like you're trying to scratch off the layers and trying to scratch off what you don't like about yourself. [*She has a rash on her face.*] Wouldn't it be easier to accept and then go deep? For without acceptance, you can't see clearly where to go, what to work on, what there is to love. [*Eight months later, a work in progress. She says, "It has come to me that we are larger than our accomplishments."*]

And there is a lot: a gentle sense of humor and love, a caring touch—you have the most wonderful touch— a kind brain, not one that seeks to make others feel bad for being who they are, a compassionate heart, a

loving manner, a quiet mind—you are the best!
Amanita, believe it! I do; you can too! There is so
much to discover about yourself, like looking at a
beautiful flower on a spring day, a first spring day of a
year, that is the kind of beauty that is held within you.
[*She is realizing she's still her, despite the sickness. Again
she states, "It's a work in progress."*]

Shoulders: spoke about earlier, but seems like there
is almost a spreading in the back, so over-rounded and
shouldered with burden and blame; self-blame is the
name of the game. [*She says her body is out of proportion, large chest that rounds shoulders.*] You blame yourself for everything. [*She had to repeat kindergarten.*]
There is no faith in another higher power or source
that this is happening as it should? [*Eight months later,
she intellectually can grasp this concept. She believes that
the reading planted seeds within her.*] Why can't you
believe it? Because if you did, you'd have to believe
your life is this way for a reason. It is. Amanita, you
are like a guardian angel in training, and if you can't
learn to guard the self and cooperate with that mind-
set, how will you get there? That is the lesson. [*I origi-
nally did not want to use the term* guardian angel *in
training with her as I have heard Caroline Myss use this
term, and wanted to make sure it was my intuition, not
some other source that was saying this. Amanita found this
one of the most memorable phrases of the reading, and that
it makes sense in kind of a "how can you love anyone if you
can't love yourself?" way. This concept resonates with her.*]

I see the neck as a hand twisting on it almost like an
Indian rope burn on the back, and twisting to the
right, always looking over your shoulder. [*She says, "It*

feels like there are 'bombs' dropping everywhere. Always looking over my shoulder to prepare." Neck pain and problems are one of the centers of pain.] Learn to look straight ahead, meditation to calm and quiet the mind/fear, and working with the intuition. Don't be afraid, gently, Sonia Choquette's *Psychic Pathway*. [*She had it sitting by her bed at the time of the reading, unread, an interesting synchronicity.*] A godsend. Get Jack Kornfield's *Inner Art of Meditation* audiotape. [*Eight months later, she "loves" Jack Kornfield and meditates three times a week.*]

See you scratching your face [*rash from Lyme disease*]. So much self-hatred. Amanita, you are not alone. There are those who love you. Learn to look at one terrific thing about yourself to love each day and focus on that. [*Eight months later, she says, "This is about learning to say I'm okay, look inside, not outside the self."*] See opening of head into brain—chemical balance is off, may need medication to correct this imbalance. Not depression, but suicidal; needs a blood test to determine if brain chemistry is off to help correct imbalance. You are not your brain. It is this chemical imbalance, not you, that makes you suicidal. [*Amanita says it is the "bug" that is Lyme disease—not depression—that makes her suicidal. It's not really her; her brain is not under her control in this area. It's like taking a poison or hallucinogen, but that it is the Lyme. She broke down in tears when I validated this for her, as she feels very few people understand this.*] Also St. John's Wort may be of help.

Amanita, beautiful being, learn to see the beauty inside and out of you; love thyself like you love no other. Receive the love that you so readily give to

others; don't turn away. You are worth loving and living; you are beautiful, smart, straight—meaning see,
you straightened up—and single—meaning single-
minded in your focus toward faith and love in the self.
Amanita, you are all of these things and more; believe
and love the self. That is all. That is everything.
Bless you.

Amanita later sent her husband, her brother-in-law, and a dear
friend for readings. When I spoke to her months later, she told me
that her husband was very eager to have a reading after listening to
her audiotape. But when I read for him, he seemed somewhat reluctant and said, "I thought this would be more like Amanita's reading."
I thought he didn't like the reading, but she said he really liked it.
The most important thing I mentioned? Remember when I told you
how weird impressions can be the best ones, and sometimes you have
to have the courage to mention them? I told him I saw him scratching his right butt cheek. We talked about his skin problems in this
area for a while. We talked about many more important things, but
for him, the accuracy of the right butt cheek was what made him
turn from a skeptic into a believer.

Amanita's brother-in-law was a very down-to-earth person who
had never had an intuitive reading. During the reading, I asked Mike
to get a liver function test and described what I saw. Instead,
the doctor felt the problem was in Mike's pancreas. However, both
Mike and his doctor were glad that he went in to check the liver,
because they found the pancreas problem instead. Several months
later, Mike called back, in tears. Although in his earlier visit, the doctor felt there was no liver problem, his liver actually had not been
checked. Mike continued to have problems and went back to the
doctor. He was diagnosed with hepatitis C, a liver disease. We
returned to his original reading to look at the emotional, mental, and

spiritual factors behind his liver problem. He still keeps in touch to tell me he is working on the issues we spoke about —he once even called to see if I could find a piece of jewelry he had lost!

Amanita's dear friend Tamar seemed to enjoy her reading. She has since sent me clients, so I was pretty sure that she was happy with our session. But Amanita said, "Tamar was furious with her reading! She called me immediately after you finished talking with her and was so angry!"

"I thought she liked her reading," I said, a little confused. "She didn't seem angry—she was very nice to me on the phone."

"Oh, she loved you. What she didn't like was that you were so accurate about her issues. She's fine now. She was just initially furious that you knew so much."

As you can see from the content of Lisa's and Amanita's readings, although I intuit physical, mental, and spiritual information, I seem to be best at discerning emotional information. That suits my clients, as that seems to be where their focus is and what helps them best. I can get other information, and I try not to get stuck if a different style comes up. For example, Mitzi's reading, which was primarily spiritual in nature, was just what she needed. Getting my ego caught up in a certain style or format would only interfere with what is best for my clients. Each day, I learn new ways to intuitively connect and communicate. I never stop learning or trying to improve. Recently, I read for a businessman and was struck by the quality of my information. It seemed surface to me, not going much deeper than the physical level. It turns out that Bob is a very private man, who did not want to go more deeply. His wife had a more in-depth reading with me, and he thanked me for respecting his privacy and his need to stay on the surface. In my early years as an intuitive, I would have felt that I hadn't done a good job on Bob's reading. As time has gone on, I've learned to let go and let readings be whatever they need to be for the client—I listen to my intuition.

PRACTICE

I am often asked, "Can anyone be intuitive?" I believe so. Again, it's just like practicing the piano: If you practice eight hours a day, you will become a pretty good pianist. If you link practice with natural ability, you might get to Carnegie Hall. Some people are "wired" to be better at one thing than another. Cal Ripken is a remarkable baseball player. Genetically, you could say it runs in his family, because his father, uncle, and brother all played professional ball. However, he has practiced and played baseball since he was a child and coupled it with a work ethic that is unstoppable. His love of the game—his passion—contributes to his success. I once read that the Ripken motto is "Don't just practice. Practice perfect." To me, this means, "Give it your best every time by practicing with full concentration and intention. When you push yourself to your top level every time, not just some of the time, your best will continue to get better."

Caroline Myss is considered to be the best medical intuitive in the world, as no one else in the field who has been tested has a higher accuracy rating (93 percent) than she. Psychic since birth, she practiced with Harvard-trained neurosurgeon C. Norman Shealy to fine-tune her skills and learn anatomy and physiology. Sure, she's fantastic—because she has enhanced her ability by practicing on six thousand clients.

I practice all the time too. One day, my friend and acupuncturist Tara came over to do a joint reading with me. She had taken my weekend workshop and had been practicing on her clients. Her father had recently had a stroke, and she wanted to help him. Because she was so close to the situation emotionally, she wanted a second intuitive opinion to clarify, validate, and reveal other perspectives. We sat at my kitchen table, focused ourselves, and began to write down our impressions. She handwrote hers; I typed mine. In about a half-hour, I had two pages of intuitive impressions. It took

Tara a few minutes longer, and she got far fewer insights. She seemed disappointed, remarking at my amazing speed and accuracy. I looked at her and laughed: "I'd better be pretty good—I practice all the time, and I do this for a living! Do you think I know one thing about sticking an acupuncture needle in someone? That's your area of expertise."

Tara realized that comparing herself to a professional health intuitive, or expecting to be as proficient in intuition as she is after nine years as an acupuncturist, is discouraging and unrealistic. Her intuitive impressions were very accurate, and devaluing her ability on the basis of comparisons could only hold back her development.

Even though I do health intuition readings professionally, I still have some areas where I need to improve. Fortunately, the right practitioners seem to come into my life when the time is right. Recently, I had been considering working with a psychiatrist to become more knowledgeable about the brain and mental disorders. Shortly thereafter, I met someone who fits this description. We are now exploring a working relationship.

I'm not only interested in health intuition for people, I am learning animal health intuition by working with a veterinarian. I have always believed that my intuitive skills could be applied to other areas. We spend a lot of time talking to our animals, but how much time do we spend listening to them? I had heard of other people who intuitively work with animals and wondered if I could apply the principles of health intuition (as I have taught you in this book) to nonhumans.

Working with the animals, I needed to remind myself of my early days as a health intuitive for people. I started out with small impressions and wasn't immediately 80 to 90 percent accurate.

Dr. Rodan is a well-read, conservative veterinarian. She would never use intuition as a substitute for care. However, the more we work together, the more she sees the value of intuition. We keep our relationship light. She jokes when I come in, "Got a 1-900 psychic case for you." I write down my impressions, and we compare her findings with mine. With time, my impressions are becoming more insightful and accurate.

My biggest success so far has been with Vanna, a Doberman pinscher whose owner, Susan, works in Dr. Rodan's office. At nine years of age, Vanna was in such dire straits that euthanasia was a possibility. She wasn't able to eat, and she was described as being lethargic and unresponsive, instead of her former keen self. As I did the reading, I came up with emotional factors at home as a piece of the puzzle, a time line of problems starting four years ago, and things in Vanna's environment that she was unhappy about that were causing her emotional distress. I hesitated to take down this information, as I wasn't sure if Susan would be open to it. Although Susan is a loving owner, it's not easy to hear that your emotional support and home environment need adjusting. But years of training as an intuitive for people have taught me that everything is important, so I suggested some things that Susan could do to change this stress at home. Additionally, Susan and Dr. Rodan were worried that Vanna might have a bleeding ulcer (there was blood in Vanna's stool), but I couldn't find it intuitively. Instead, I came up with some other physical symptoms. Susan validated all but one intuitive impression as correct: She said that there was no problem in Vanna's upper jaw above the left canine.

Even though I had been concerned about how some of the more personal impressions would be received, Susan took all of my information with gratitude. With nothing left to lose, and with Dr. Rodan's agreement, Susan tried my suggestions for easing Vanna's emotional strain by shifting her home environment, supplementing her diet with B vitamins and herbal remedies, and giving her massages. Additionally, she scheduled an upper gastrointestinal "scope" to check for the presence of the ulcer (it found nothing, as did I). Within a few weeks, Susan noticed an improvement in Vanna's emotional state.

A few weeks later, Vanna was feeling so much better that Susan decided to get Vanna's teeth cleaned. Although she was nine, and many dogs need their teeth cleaned by this time, Vanna did not have a lot of tartar and she had no telltale bad breath. Based on her age, and the accuracy of my other intuitive impressions, Susan decided to do the dental cleaning anyway. She encouraged Dr. Rodan, "Make sure you check those canines—Karen said she thought there was something in the upper jaw above one of them." Dr. Rodan wiggled the left tooth. "Wiggle harder," Susan said. The tooth broke off in Dr. Rodan's hand, revealing a large abscess up into the upper jaw. Because of its size, Dr. Rodan felt the abscess must have been bothering Vanna for quite some time, yet there were no outward signs. She later said, "It's not like they can tell you what's wrong with them." I smiled at her and said, "Sure they can. Want to take my class on intuitive development?" She just grinned.

Susan reported that after two weeks' time, Vanna had regressed five years in attitude and physical health. She is back to her old, loving self with good health. I feel such incredible joy and gratitude that one of the "silent creatures" was heard and helped through intuition. On a side note, after I finished my reading with Vanna, I met her in the flesh. She was testy with me, as she was with other people. After all of her treatments had been completed, we met again. This time I got lots of cuddles and kisses—my favorite reward.

Working with animals has reinforced to me how unlimited my intuition can be as long as I give it the right focus and practice. Recently, I had a dream that I would use my intuition to help at archeological digs. As a student and a teacher, I am constantly evolving, and you will too.

I've taught my health intuition method to everyone from M.D.s and Ph.D.s to bodyworkers to regular people, like my mom. *Intuitive* is not the first word that comes to mind in describing my mom. She still lives in my conservative hometown with my dad. She is retired, grows flowers, volunteers, shops, and is a housewife. She took my class so she could tune in to her one-year-old granddaughter. Perfect. Everyone has different goals and aspirations. We might not all end up at Carnegie Hall, giving an intuitive recital; we may just need to "listen" to a little child who has not yet learned to use words. Like Cal Ripken, Caroline Myss, a concert pianist—or like me, who had no innate health intuitive ability—you need to practice to get anywhere in life. The same goes for intuition.

PEEKING

Is it okay to "peek" at people—to read them without their knowing it? What do you think? Ponder for a moment before you read on. My classes seem to be split on this one. Some people say it's not appropriate to use your intuition to check out other people without their permission. I agree. I come from a long line of nosy people; for no good reason, we seem to be interested in what everyone else is doing. As I became noticeably intuitive, I realized how distracting it was to me to know things that were of no use to me. It's enough to live my own life—why would I fill up my time and brain space with clutter? There is also the issue of integrity. It did not feel right. For a long time, I refused to use my intuitive skills in interviewing and hiring situations. Some of my friends pointed out that I would certainly use my hearing (or my other senses) to listen and learn about someone. They argued that, logically, it was unreasonable for me not to use my sixth sense as well. It even could be argued that people being interviewed were giving their permission to be checked out. In public, many spiritual figures invite people to look at their selves and their lives, to observe what it is to lead an exemplary life. They want people to learn from their example.

I agreed that all these arguments were logical; still, I resisted. One night, I had a most vibrant and colorful dream. In my dream, I was to do a conference recording of the Dalai Lama, the spiritual leader of the Tibetan people. Clothed in a bright monk's robe, he was sitting under a big tree, on the greenest grass I have ever seen. I said, "Your microphone, Your Holiness." He took it, smiling, saying nothing. Then in my dream, I thought, *This is your chance! Check him out. See what this example of a spiritual person's energy system looks like.* I closed my eyes for a moment and looked. A tear rolled down my cheek. It was so beautiful. I opened my eyes, and His Holiness said, "All my children are this beautiful"—he paused—"in their own way."

He said nothing further. I did not feel chastised for peeking. Instead, I felt that I was to look upon other beings' energy with respect and see the divinity and beauty within each. At the time of my dream, I knew very little of the Dalai Lama. Since then, I have learned that his message is one of compassion. My dream seemed to convey that perfectly.

That day, I told a co-worker about my dream. "Great," he said. "We have an enlightened spiritual leader—a guru—recording in the studio. You can check her out."

"No, no, I couldn't do that," I replied, still stuck in my old way of thinking.

"Remember your dream," he said.

Later that day, the recording studio editor came into my office. To my amazement, he invited me to come into the studio to hear the guru, who was visiting from India. In the two years I had worked there, I had never been asked to view a recording in progress. As I walked in, the guru was chanting. I closed my eyes, sat still, and looked at her energy. I saw little circles spinning inside her, lined up in a vertical row, in sync with one another, and beautifully colored in the order of the hues of a rainbow. As I finished intuiting, I imagined that I was bowing to her beautiful energy. As I opened my eyes, she looked right at me and physically bowed her head as she continued chanting. She knew! Even though I gave no outward sign of what I was doing, she was aware.

What were those little spinning things? I had no idea. I called my spiritual mentor, George, into my office. I drew little pinwheels on a stick figure and exclaimed, "Her chakra energy centers were moving! Like a pinwheel! In color!"

He laughed and said, "*Chakra* means 'wheel' in Sanskrit. You've been looking at too many Americans who don't have a spiritual practice. This is what someone who has a balanced spiritual practice looks like."

I now believe that if I am meant to read someone—to learn from them—I am able to see what needs to be seen. I do not see any more than that, as I ask for the information as "the truth, so that they can hear it and it can help them." I do not intuit to be nosy, for no reason. I do use intuition in my business and my personal life when it feels appropriate.

Over the years, I have had clients for whom I am unable to read. When this first happened, I was upset. Ankara met me at one of my classes and made an appointment for a reading. She asked excellent questions during the workshop, and I looked forward to our time together. As usual, on the day of her reading, I tuned in ahead of time. Nothing came. Nothing. Nothing. Six times I tried; six times, not a speck of information came. I felt embarrassed, upset, and disappointed. I phoned her and gave her the news. She was so gracious: "Karen, I really like you, and I loved the class. But I changed my mind about the reading. It's not the right time for me. You were so nice; I didn't know how to tell you that I didn't want a reading right now. This works out perfectly."

Ankara had rescinded her permission, and without even knowing it in my thinking mind, my intuition did the right thing. From then on, whenever I have been unable to conduct a reading for someone, I trust that it is meant to be. All the clients to whom this has happened have been equally as gracious as Ankara. Some are unsure why they cannot be read, but they trust that it is meant to be. One client said she thought she was a "psychic junkie," consulting an intuitive before every decision. She believed that my inability to read her was a message telling her to start relying more on herself. Whatever the reason the client comes up with, it seems to be right that no reading comes at that time. Some clients try again later. Some I can read for; some I still cannot. I think it may have something to do with the right time, the right place, and the right person. There also have been times when a client is in a big hurry for a reading, but our appointment schedules do not coincide, or some force of nature interferes. When the reading finally happens, it's often clear that the delay was for a reason. The person may have needed those few weeks to go through some meaningful experiences, or a big shift was about to take place and a reading was more appropriate later. These situations invariably leave us both feeling that "everything is happening as it should." I have learned to trust that the right thing will happen.

If my intuition is not there, and I am not meant to get a reading, I have enough faith and experience to know that overriding a "no-reading" impression is not in anyone's best interest. I have learned not to force my intuition; however, I can turn it off and on. Early in my exploration of this skill, George suggested that I use a visualization to help me do this, maybe something from my childhood. When I was a little girl, there was a television show called *My Favorite Martian*. Whenever the martian wanted to use his special powers, his antennae came up. They went back down when he wanted to act like a normal human being. It may sound silly, but it's more fun to play with intuition than to work it, so I initially used this image to help me set boundaries. Now that I'm more experienced, I don't have to use this visualization to turn my intuition off and on. Some intuitives do not use boundaries. They are so comfortable and experienced at always being on and filtering—it is such a part of their "I am"—that they don't set parameters. Most people, including me, are not entirely at ease being intuitively on all the time. You can develop a ritual, an invocation, or an image to use when you want to tune in. And you can "just say no" to intuitive impressions that are not comfortable for you. Go with what is right for you.

ASKING QUESTIONS

Although I would like to tell you that with my intuition I can win the lottery (and teach you how to do so as well), alas, it is not meant to be. One day, I asked my intuition, "Can I play the lottery?" The answer was yes, so I excitedly bought a ticket. The numbers I picked were not even close. Amazed, I asked about my losing lotto experience. My intuition seemed to laugh at me, as the answer I received was, "You can play all you want, but it's not your destiny to win!" I could have saved myself a dollar if I had asked a better question to begin with. Oh, well. Albert Einstein knew the value was in the question: "It's more important to know what the problem is than to find the solution, because stating the problem correctly often leads almost automatically to the solution."[4] The receiving part of the intuitive process is easy—it's the question part that takes the most practice. The better the questions, the better your answers.

Sandra Ingerman is a famous shaman and teacher. She tells how countless students write to her along these lines: "I asked my guidance if I should marry this person. It said, yes. I married him [or her], and four years later, we are divorced!" The student might have been better off asking an open-ended question. The answer may have been yes because it was important for the student to learn from this person or for some other reason. By asking open-ended questions, you get the details.

I teach my students to be "energy journalists." In high school, when I took Journalism I, I learned that a good reporter asks the "five Ws and the one H": who, what, when, where, why, and how are the essential questions to get to the crux of any situation. Taking the "Should I marry this person?" example a bit further, you might ask open-ended questions such as these:

"*Whom* should I marry?"

"*What* will be the outcome if I marry this person?"

"*When* would be the best time for me to marry?"

"*Where* might I find a person with the qualities needed to give me a long-term, happy relationship?"

"*Why* would I marry this person?"

"*How* should I go about finding a marriage partner?"

You can be an energy journalist with any intuitive need or impression. If you get a visual flash, hear some words you don't understand, or have a feeling that doesn't make sense, *ask*. For example, "What are you trying to tell me? Please put it in a way I will understand." Or use any of the other five Ws and one H to give you greater clarity.

Being an energy journalist serves another important purpose. Since the left side of the brain is the analytical side, and the right side is the seat of intuition, the left side may be overdeveloped and stronger. My first thirty years seem to have been spent in so much left-brained, analytical thinking that I wonder sometimes why my head is not lopsided. For myself, and for many of my students, the left brain is so powerful that the intuitive right side can hardly be heard. Additionally, the left side may feel threatened by "the new kid on the block"—intuition. Can you recall a time at school or at work where you worked very hard and were doing a great job? Then someone new came aboard, and you felt insecure wondering if they would eclipse you. Eventually, you found that the new person was a great help or maybe even became a good friend. This same kind of thinking extends to your brain. Silly as it may sound, I suggest having a talk with your left side: "Left side, you have worked so hard, for so many years, all by yourself, with little or no support. Wouldn't you like some help? A vacation or break from time to time? Intuition will not take over for you, only be of great help and support. What do you think?"

This simple dialogue really seems to offer reassurance to the busy left side and helps you be a more balanced being, using both sides of your brain. When you are intuiting, give your left side a task. That way, it is less likely to interfere or feel left out. The left side gets to be the energy journalist, to ask the really great questions. Tell your left side you have a new job for it, and see what excellent results you will have as you ask better questions each time you intuit. A lot of my students are health professionals. They feel they have a big hurdle to overcome. Not only is their left side powerful and skilled, it is full of medical knowledge. They sometimes wonder if their impressions are based on their education or on intuition. I tell them that it really doesn't matter, as long as they get accurate and helpful information. However, there are ways to find out.

Beulah is a massage therapist who took my weekend workshop. Immediately, she put what she learned into practice by tuning in to new clients before their initial meeting. When the clients arrived for their first appointment, she verified her impressions by having them fill out a health history and interviewing them. She believed she could not do this with her old clients, as she "knew too much." One day, she was stuck. A client of many years, Mildred, was at a plateau in the healing process. Beulah tuned in, got some information, and shared it with Mildred. It was right on. It was something Beulah had no way of knowing and Mildred had not considered. Brought to light and treated, it moved Mildred out of her stuck place and toward improved health and healing.

Joshua is a holistic medical doctor. It is important to him to know if his thoughts represent intuition or acquired knowledge. He simply has his left brain ask, "Where is this knowledge coming from?"

BEGINNER'S MIND

My students are right: The beginner's mind can be a blessing. I sometimes struggle doing a reading when one client reminds me of another person. I recently read for Ivan, a man from the former Soviet Union. He reminded me so much of a former roommate's father, Vasil, that I mixed the two of them up. As a result, my only two inaccuracies in the reading (according to Ivan) were his weight and his hair. I got impressions about both, but instead of asking for further information on these issues, I superimposed Vasil (whom I have seen in person), who is overweight and losing his hair, over Ivan (whom I had not seen), who is underweight and has a head full of hair. When I was a beginner, I went more slowly while doing readings. As I became more practiced as an intuitive, I found myself going too fast, jumping to conclusions—as I did with Ivan—and coming up with incorrect assumptions (there's that word again) and interpretations. Now I am more careful: I rely on my experience, but I still try to retain the good qualities from my early days—carefulness and mindfulness. If I am unsure about something, I ask my intuition, instead of assuming.

Perhaps you are reading this book, thinking, *I don't have any experience with this intuition stuff. This will be impossible.*

Loren came to my workshop with his wife, Sally. She had been medically intuitive for years and worked in a health care setting. She was very excited to hear about my work. For Valentine's Day, Loren agreed to accompany Sally to my workshop, and she agreed to go fishing with him the following weekend. Loren described himself as a businessman who liked to play golf and tennis. He had no previous experience or interest in health intuition. To this day, I am shocked and amazed when I think about that workshop in Los Angeles. I have never had a student, before or since, who has had such an incredible number of hits on the first exercise. As Loren focused on the person the class was reading, he accurately ascertained a variety of issues and health problems. His hits were greater than the cumulative total of the rest of the class. To say that Sally and I and the other students (including an M.D.) were impressed does not convey the magnitude of the situation. Loren is an example of how the beginner's mind can be a great aid to intuition. It worked for him, and it can work for you too.

INTUITION OR EMOTION?

How can you tell if the impressions you are getting are coming from your intuition, your emotion, or your projection of what you want to happen? Again, getting the left side of the brain out of the way of your intuitive right side will help. Remember to give your left side a job: let it ask questions and be the energy journalist. In my classes, I offer this example, which you can do right now: Pretend you are in my class. I take the cap off my water bottle and hold it up. I ask if there is anyone who absolutely must have my water bottle cap. "Is there anyone here who really wants this? Can't live without it?" No one has ever raised a hand. Nobody cares. They feel neutral about it. It does not matter. Then I take a piece of paper with some writing on it. I say: "This is a letter from the only person who ever broke off a relationship with you and did not give you complete closure. This letter explains everything, and you will feel at peace and complete when you read it." Some members of the audience giggle and smile. Others become somber and thoughtful.

What do you feel when I talk about my water bottle cap? Probably nothing much. Examine your feelings about the letter, however. How do you feel about it? Do memories come up? Do you imagine what that person looks like? Can you see his face, hear her voice? Do you feel funny somewhere (or everywhere) in your body? Look at the difference between these two sets of feelings. They are very different, and you can gauge them. Intuition is like the first one, neutral. I think of it as a gentle breeze on a summer day: if you are not paying attention, you might miss it. The letter has an entirely different charge, or feeling, to it. That is emotion.

Everyone's intuitive hits will have a unique quality. Learn to recognize how your intuition feels, and you will increase your accuracy. Your special feeling of correct intuition will be different from mine, your neighbor's, or your best friend's. It will be uniquely your own. Recognizing that feeling—and learning to act on it—is the key to using intuition. Each time you intuit and get a hit, remember how it feels. Remember how a miss feels too. Think back to how it felt when you just *knew* where that parking space was. Next time, look for that quality of feeling, and see if you can score another great parking place.

When I first started as a health intuitive, I worked with a doctor who practiced on the East Coast of the United States. Via phone, she gave me approximately twenty names and ages of patients. I was to type up a reading for each and mail them to her. When I got a little more than halfway through, I got a strange feeling with number fourteen. I had no idea what this feeling was about. I thought there might be something seriously wrong with the person, so I contacted the physician's office. It turned out that I had the client's name wrong: It was Kathleen *Mills*, not *Hills*. I had discovered the importance of the intuitive quality of feeling. I was out of the flow—the person did not exist, so my intuition felt funny, or off-kilter. The more you practice, the more you will know what it feels like to have an intuitive impression that is right on. Paying attention to these feelings helps to increase your accuracy.

CHAPTER 13

Tuning In

It's time to try out your intuition. The basics I've mentioned in previous chapters can help you with intuition in everyday situations, and they apply to health intuition as well. We're going to focus on doing a health reading. Remain very playful; just try it on yourself and see if you like it. I like the expression "Fake it 'til you make it"; some of my students prefer "*Faith* it 'til you make it." Either way, just try it out, playfully; if you're not sure this is for real, just have fun and pretend. Also, keep in mind what I've taught you about intuition. While I've made most of these discoveries one by one, you get the payoff from years of detective work!

Which impressions are best? In many people's experience (mine included) the ones that are quick, first, subtle, and unusual. The more *quickly* you go, the less time there is for your left brain to get in the way. *First* impressions not only help you to be quick, but also they are usually right-brain intuitive impressions—they arrive before your imagination or intellect has time to come up with something that makes sense to the analytical left brain. *Subtle* impressions usually have to do with the soft "voice" (or visual impression or feeling) that our intuition has, especially early on. *Unusual* is a key to knowing intuition or imagination and intellect. Usually imagination and intellect follow a logical course. An unusual insight may not be logical (at least not at first look), or it can seem like a surprise, out of nowhere. Make a note of it, and keep intuiting. You can always check out those surprising and unusual insights later, with your intellect, after you're finished intuiting. Many times, you'll find that these impressions are right on and end up making perfect sense.

As I discussed in chapter 12, you may receive impressions in any of three ways: audio, visual, or kinesthetic. An audio impression is that little voice in your head. An example of a visual impression is closing your eyes and seeing your bedroom in your "mind's eye." A kinesthetic impression is anything you may feel in your body: pain, a smell, a vibration, and so on. These impressions are referred to as clairaudient (clear hearing), clairvoyant (clear seeing), and clairsentient (clear sensing). But don't get caught up in labels; just go with the flow.

THE HEALTH INTUITION THREE-STEP PROCESS

Here are the steps I lead my health intuition classes through. I like to keep the intuition process simple, so it's only a three-step process: meditate, invocate, tune in.

Step 1: Meditate

Don't get caught up in labels. Quieting the mind, contemplating, focusing your attention, concentrating on your breath—all are ways to meditate. Intuition, especially in the beginning, competes poorly with other stimulation, so relaxation and focus are important. In my classes, we get in the habit of relaxing ourselves quickly. We focus on five cycles of breath (breathing in and out once is one cycle). Make sure your feet are firmly planted on the ground as you breathe—you want to feel grounded instead of "flaky" or ungrounded in your intuition. Some days, you may feel the need to breathe or meditate longer. Do what you need to do.

Step 2: Invocate

A copy of the invocation I use and an explanation of each of the components can be found on pages 160–167. You can use mine or make up one of your own.

Step 3: Tune In

The final step in this process is to tune in to your body. Some of my students close their eyes for this step; others keep them open. Starting at the bottom of your body, move upward, step-by-step. To begin with, think *Feet*. Pause and wait for a quick impression; write it down. *Ankles*. Pause and write. Continue up through your entire body. A worksheet is included in the appendix for your use (pages 225–226). It is important to write down or record your impressions, so you will remember them.

If you would like to make a recording to guide you through your body, simply read the worksheet aloud into a tape recorder. Play it each time you tune in.

INVOCATION

_____, *please give me the information on*
(Divine source)
_____. *The truth so*
(name and age or whatever information you may have)
that they can hear it and it can help them. Please let this
information come through with compassion, clarity, and, if
appropriate, completeness, the cause behind the cause,
through my heart center.

Please do not let anything of mine (filters, biases, assump-
tions, etc.) interfere with the message.

I ask that none of my vital energy be used in obtaining this
information.

Please send a blessing to _____.
(person for whom you are reading)
Thank you.

COMPONENTS OF THE INVOCATION

This is the invocation I use. I'll discuss each component so you can determine its relevance to your needs and preferences.

Divine source,
Use any words you want here. Some ideas might include *heavenly father, divine mother, universe, God, Buddha, higher power, spirit, guidance, divine energy, higher self, source.* I think it is important to hold the intention to plug into the highest source possible in order to gather the purest information.

Please give me the information on_____ (name and age or whatever information you may have).
You can use anything to focus your attention: a photo, first name only, an address, the actual person, something he or she has touched. Do not get caught up in my personal preference (name and age), because that could get in the way of your own intuitive process. I use name and age, as that is the technique the first intuitive I met used. I know one intuitive who is so superstitious that he believes he can only read people at his special desk, with a certain kind of paper and pen. I suggest that you use anything that's available, and be flexible. I once did a reading using a folded piece of paper with the person's name and age on it. I was not allowed to see the information on the paper. The result? It was quite accurate for the client, and empowering and confidence building for me.

The truth so that they can hear it and it can help them.
Truth is of no use if it cannot be heard or be of help. Truth changes, depending on many factors. Using this phrase, you can tune in to what works *right now.* The wording also seems to perform a censoring capability, giving my clients pertinent information in the present

moment. I once asked for "the truth" with no modifications. The results were disastrous. The man kept denying that it was he I was talking about. His parents were wonderful, his family was perfect, and so on. At the end of the reading, though, he decided it could be his younger (by eighteen months) brother whom I was speaking about. I asked him, "So your parents were wonderful to you, your family is perfect from your perspective, but your brother, who is nearly the same age as you, had a totally different experience?" I asked the questions out of curiosity, wanting to understand what he was saying to me, not to say, "I'm right and you're wrong." He thought for a few minutes, and really had no answer. He felt this was something he needed to ponder. Months later I received word from a third party that he was surprised with the accuracy of the information, that it hit him too hard, and that he could only deny as a defense mechanism.

I use the unisex term *they* for two reasons. First, I don't always know a client's gender when I invoke. Second, I don't want to have to take the time to remember particulars about the person once I am into the invocation. I feel like that engages my intellectual left-brain side instead of letting my intuitive right brain flow.

Perhaps the following visual image will help you see how "the truth" can be too powerful. In archery competition, if someone strikes the bull's-eye dead center, one must look from an angle to be able to see the arrow. The same is true with truth. That is why I ask for the truth so that clients can hear it, and it will help them. This does not mean I abdicate all common sense when communicating to clients. For example, as a session with a client progresses, he or she may become very emotional and vulnerable. I like to double-check with my intuition if I get a feeling during the reading that the language may be a little too direct. My intuition can then give me softer words to use. Otherwise, I feel comfortable that the information coming through is right for the client, now, and it is my job to diplomatically share it.

Please let this information come through with compassion . . . through my heart center.

When you were a child, did a teacher or other adult ever yell at you when you had made a mistake? How did you feel? Before reading further, recall the experience. Most people close down and cannot hear a message when it is screamed at them. Some people like to receive information in a very blunt manner. These people need to find another intuitive to work with, as that is not my style. Information in a reading is very personal. For it to be of most benefit, I need people to be able to hear it and feel comfortable with it. This is why I present it with kindness and love. I hold the intention to use my heart center to work as a receiver and transmitter. I get the words that go heart-to-heart, from me to my client. This gentle approach seems to get the message across more than any show of power, abrasive directness, or voice raising.

. . . clarity, and, if appropriate, completeness, the cause behind the cause . . .
It's not appropriate for everyone to know everything in their lives— where would be the fun of discovering? Some people are ready for more complete information. For others, just a little goes a long way. Divine order needs to unfold at different rates for different people. Asking for clarity helps me to be more accurate in receiving and conveying the information. I do not withhold information that is meant for the client, but sometimes I receive information only for me. For example, John consulted me for a reading. As I began the reading, my intuition said, "Karen, know that he is an undiagnosed schizophrenic. Make sure you reiterate many times that he needs psychotherapeutic help, but do not label him. He will try to draw you into his web of intrigue. Stick to the reading and don't get caught up in chitchat." I followed the guidance I was given and the reading proceeded smoothly, in spite of John's efforts to distract me from the business at hand.

I once attended a workshop given by another medical intuitive and a doctor. They presented some case studies together. In a typical one, the medical intuitive was given the name and age of the client. She reported to the doctor, "Something in the throat area and the pelvis." The doctor ran tests and found thyroid and ovarian problems. One of the workshop attendees asked the doctor if he would prefer that the intuitive be more specific to save time and money and to better serve the patient. He replied, "No—I have a medical degree and a brain. I can figure out what's wrong with the patient!"

This pair seemed uninterested in getting to other components—mental, emotional, or spiritual—of the physical manifestation. After the presentation, several workshop attendees voiced the opinion that because the doctor was seeing forty-five patients a day, perhaps he was more interested in running people through his practice and making money on extra tests. This is a possibility, but we may never really know his motivations. Many people in the audience felt deeply unsatisfied that this duo was addressing symptoms only, instead of getting to the root of the problem.

Without exception, every health care professional I have worked with and spoken to believes that getting to the cause is extremely helpful in working toward health, healing, and well-being. These are busy people. They want to know what's wrong with their patients, specifically. They find that the time saved through using their own intuition, or consulting an intuitive who is specific, is very helpful. Doing this does not insult their egos or devalue their education.

One last note on the relationship between this doctor and the medical intuitive: I think it is perfectly fine that this doctor preferred not to work with an intuitive who is very specific. Although their style is different from mine, their relationship works for them, and if it helps patient care, it is a wonderful thing.

Please do not let anything of mine (filters, biases, assumptions, etc.) interfere with the message.
Without impediments, the message is clearer and there is less interference from the left brain and your own biases.

I ask that none of my vital energy be used in obtaining this information.
There is never a need to feel drained when using your energy to do a reading. By tapping into the divine source, you experience an unlimited and untainted energy supply. This piece is extremely important. Since I've used it in my invocation, I have not felt tired or experienced any body reactions to doing this work. Many intuitives burn out, or become overweight, through taking on clients' "stuff." When I mention this in workshops, the students often tease me, telling me I might do well to take on a little extra weight (I am thin for my height). I feel refreshed when I do readings. This step is simple and it works.

Optional: Please send a blessing to (person for whom you are reading).
Everything in the invocation is optional. You can decide for yourself whether to include any piece I've suggested. I send each client, and every inhabitant of our earth, a blessing when I do a reading. I simply say, "Bless you." This is an open-ended blessing, just like the one given when someone sneezes. I think it's a nice thing to do.

Thank you.
Gratitude is a wonderful habit to cultivate—I believe it builds positive energy. When I view a grateful person's health system, I can see a huge difference in the way they feel and are able to deal with life. I make gratitude a habit in the readings and in my personal life too.

My invocation is constantly evolving. Yours will too. Recently, I was very tired and had a full week of readings in front of me. I simply added to my invocation, "Please revitalize me with your divine energy." After the first reading, I felt much better. Now, on the rare occasions when I get to bed late and am concerned I will be tired the next day, I request that I feel rested and refreshed, in spite of the shortened sleep cycle. It seems to work. Another day, I felt that I was struggling and having a hard time receiving insights. I simply added to my invocation, "Please let the impressions come with grace and ease." It worked well, and I decided to request grace and ease whenever I was struggling. It took me a few weeks to figure out that I could ask for grace and ease every time. (Sometimes I'm a bit of a slow learner!)

Even though I teach intuition, sometimes I need to be personally reminded of things I stress to my students. Seven months ago, I started experiencing incredible right-knee pain. I asked my intuition and received two messages: "slow down" and "stop using that ergonomic chair." I began to slow down my speed in life matter, and in simple ways like walking slower and meditating more. I stopped using the chair, too, but the pain persisted. I consulted an osteopath for treatment and received some relief. I intuited again, and got another message relating to inner work. I worked on it for many months and experienced improvement in my knee. But there was still some pain. I got one more emotional message and worked on that component too. After all of this inner work, I then intuitively heard, "See an acupuncturist." I usually dress pretty casually around the house, in socks or bare feet. The morning of my acupuncture appointment, I needed to leave the house as soon as I'd finished a reading. So, dressed and ready to go (shoes and all), I sat down to tune in to my client. I felt uncomfortable, so I kicked off my shoes and put my feet firmly on the ground with the sudden realization, *I really need my feet to be in touch with the ground when I read for people.* After the reading, I mentioned to my husband, "I just noticed I really need foot contact with the ground when I read for people." He replied, "Isn't that what you teach your students? To be grounded?" I had to admit that I was teaching them one thing, but forgot to do it for me! He then told me about a native tribe in South America that refuses to wear shoes because they believe contact with the ground is so important. I went to the acupuncturist, and he asked if I had changed chairs lately. I told him all about the ergonomic chair being part of the start of my knee problem. He explained that in Chinese medicine, energy—or life force—gets stuck. He believed that when I do my readings, I need the energy to flow throughout my body. By sitting with my knee bent and with my entire body weight on it, I wasn't touching the ground. As a result, the energy got stuck and caused pain. I told him about my insight just that morning, when I had to kick my shoes off to read for my client (talk about synchronicity) and he mentioned the same South American tribe that my husband had referred to earlier. My knee is fine. Now, I ground myself every time I do a reading by planting my feet firmly on the floor and feel the energy flow, with no negative repercussions.

Consider grounding yourself, using an invocation, and personalizing it according to your needs. It offers numerous benefits and eliminates some of the drawbacks of intuitive work.

AFTER YOUR FIRST READING

When you are finished intuiting, shake off the energy. Shake your hands out or wash them. (I wash my hands and arms up to my elbows.) Perform some ritual, or state the intention that you are shaking off the energy, keeping only that which is your own, giving nothing away. You may think, *Why do I need to shake off my own energy?* Shaking off the energy helps you to shift from a very intuitive state to a more integrated state for real-world living. It also sets up a good habit for each time you read, whether for yourself or others.

Give yourself some feedback. Look over your impressions and consider what their meaning might be. If you are unsure, go back in. Be an energy journalist (ask *who, what, when, where, why,* or *how*) and get more information. If you find something that frightens you, remember: You are new at this, and you could be wrong. Or you could be right, so get checked by your health care professional. Remember, always consult your health care practitioner before making any changes in your health care regimen.

As you were reading yourself (tuning in to your "check engine" lights), did you try to write down the first, quick insights, especially the strange ones? Did you remember that impressions can come in any form—audio, visual, or kinesthetic? If not, that's fine. It's your first reading; with practice, it will come to you. Avoid assumption by *describing* what you see, hear, or intuitively feel instead of interpreting it. Pay attention to how you feel when you are receiving intuitive impressions—as I did when I noticed a difference between Kathleen Mills and Kathleen Hills—so you begin to learn the difference between intuition and emotion.

When I first started this work, I had a great deal of trouble remembering what I had just intuited. Because I am a skeptic by nature, I thought this was a sign that I was faking it, even though clients gave me the feedback that I was accurate. I have an excellent memory. I remember trivial facts as well as anyone I have ever met, and I harbor a secret wish to be on the television show *Jeopardy* to test my knowledge. In light of the fact that my memory is so good, I was confused when I could not remember the content of the readings. Jumping to conclusions, my skeptical mind decided that this was evidence that I was not intuitive. I asked a friend, a professional intuitive, about this dilemma:

"Even though my readings seem to be accurate, I can't remember their content. Do you think I'm faking it?" I asked.

She said, "No. I think that's a brilliant sign."

It was not until I read Valerie Hunt's *Infinite Mind*[1] that I understood what she meant. Hunt has studied intuitives at the University of California at Los Angeles. Through her work at UCLA, she discovered that psychics shift brain-wave states while intuiting. The ordinary waking state for most people is the alpha brain-wave state. When we sleep deeply, we move into delta. When we are in an intuitive or inspirational and creative state, we are in theta. You can liken the theta/intuitive state to a sleep state in which you have a hard time remembering the content of your dreams when you wake up. I do not go into a trance when I am conducting a reading; however, I am very focused and easily startled. By recording my impressions, I have a record of what I intuited in the theta brain-wave state, so that I can refer to it when I'm in alpha—when I'm speaking to a client or doing everyday tasks.

Remember, take time to practice your intuition whenever you get the chance, not just in health matters, but in everyday situations. Even though I'm a professional health intuitive, I probably spend only about 10 percent of my time intuiting about health. The rest of the time, I live a normal, everyday life. Therefore, it makes sense for me to use intuition throughout my day, on everyday things. It helps me to be a better intuitive, overall, and since I'm spending 90 percent of my time in the real world, I might as well take advantage of it— and so can you. So take a cue from my student who asked and listened to her intuition at every opportunity: How much will my groceries be? My gas? Which is the best route? Where will I find a parking space? The variations are as endless and creative as you are. Practice, practice, practice and hold the right intention. You'll get there.

CHAPTER 14

Methods of Intuiting

For a while, I thought there was only one medical intuitive on the planet. Unaware of others, I thought Caroline Myss had invented a totally new profession. As I have grown, I have learned that she is a modern pioneer, but there are others too. Here is some background on the systems that have been most helpful to my development and how they interplay with my health intuition method. Consider looking into the Myss and Brennan methods, which I will describe in this chapter, or finding other teachers and systems to augment your learning. More teachers are coming out of the woodwork all of the time. Keep your eyes open for their books and workshops.

THE MYSS METHOD (CHAKRA SYSTEM)

Caroline Myss holds a Ph.D. in energy medicine and intuition. The first physician she worked with was C. Norman Shealy, M.D., Ph.D. For more than fifteen years, they have partnered in research, creating the terms *medical intuition* and *medical intuitive*, as well as writing and speaking about the field. The public scope of their work is unparalleled in the field, and they are both pioneers in bringing this health/medical intuition closer to being a legitimate profession by setting a standard of accuracy and providing an example of a working relationship between a medical professional and an intuitive.

In the preface to her book *Anatomy of the Spirit*, Myss states that in the fall of 1982, "I gradually recognized that my perceptual abilities had expanded considerably. For instance, a friend would mention that someone he knew was not feeling well, and an insight into the cause of the problem would pop into my head. . . . By the spring of 1983 I was doing readings for people who were in health crises and life crises of various kinds."[1]

Although she had credentials as a journalist and publisher, and a master's degree in theology, Myss lacked a medical background with which to couple her intuitive skill. Eventually she met Dr. Shealy, a Harvard-trained neurosurgeon, and he began to give her names and ages of patients to read intuitively. Long-distance, she would give him her impressions. As time went on, Shealy trained her in the language of anatomy, so that she had a professional vocabulary with which to describe her intuitive sensations. Shealy found her readings to be 93 percent accurate. Myss successfully shifted her career focus from intuiting for individuals to teaching and writing. *Anatomy of the Spirit* rose to number six on the *New York Times* best-seller list. She is an extremely popular speaker on the lecture circuit, and her audio- and videotapes are top sellers.

Myss calls the language of her impressions "energy" and "symbolic sight." In her audiotape *Energy Anatomy*,[2] she details her major beliefs and a system of cataloging ill health. She asserts that certain illnesses relate to specific belief structures that are held within cellular memory in the body. Specifically located, these areas affect body and disease states. Myss categorizes these areas by using the chakra system of energy vortices within the body. According to ancient Hindi knowledge, there are seven major chakras in the body. The first chakra is located in the sacral area (tailbone) of the physical body and projects out into the energy body (energy that projects outside the body, but follows its form and gives information on health and other issues). This is the "tribal" chakra. It holds beliefs about any group one belongs to, for example, a family, a club, a place of work, a nationality. Within the energy body, the second chakra is located in the pelvic area; the third, in the solar plexus; the fourth, in the heart; the fifth, in the throat; the sixth, in the forehead (third-eye area); and the seventh, on the crown of the head. Myss believes that each chakra contains different issues. She is of the opinion that ill health can be created from beliefs that are draining or damaging as well as past traumas. Myss maintains that by dealing with these issues, one can attain greater well-being.

In another audio recording, *Why People Don't Heal*,[3] Myss explains two other important concepts discovered through her work as a medical intuitive. "Woundology" is a language that many cultures, including American, use to meet and bond with others. According to Myss, a small wound bonding might be "You never got cookies as a kid? I never got cupcakes!" People use bigger wounds as "currency" to excuse behaviors, receive sympathy, and gain attention from others. Eventually, this wound-reliance can result in ill health, because these beliefs drain instead of energize the body. The second concept— "how your biography becomes your biology"—postulates that memories, resentments, regrets, and other negative attitudes that are held onto for many years can eventually fester into various "dis-ease" states. In private conversations I have had with Myss about how she gathers information, she told me that she primarily feels different qualities of vibration. Through years of experience and several thousand readings, she has learned to recognize each vibration as it correlates with a particular disease state, symptom, or issue.

Myss is not the only medical intuitive to base her intuitive impressions on this method. Her ideas and research formed the foundation for my work as a health intuitive. I believe that Myss's work, along with that of many other trailblazers, is a large part of the reason I have achieved success in this field.

THE HEALTH INTUITION METHOD

Some of my students prefer working with the chakra system only, and not some other system, such as mine or Barbara Brennan's. I also started out using Myss's technique, but over time the chakras have almost completely disappeared as my means of gathering intuitive information. The information just seems to flow for me now. I liken it to a book, where all the chapters are needed to tell the whole story. Sometimes people want a short reading, because they are in a hurry. Or a TV or radio host will ask me to do "three-minute readings" on people. I say no to these requests, as it takes up to an hour for me to impart the intuitive information contained in a reading to a client. I give them the whole book so to speak; I don't just pull out chapters one and nine. How could anyone get the complete meaning of a book by reading just two chapters? You might have some idea of the content, but not a full understanding.

Valerie Hunt, Ed.D.,[4] articulated the way I now intuitively evaluate. I believe that I am accessing energy fields instead of chakras. Chakras feel more compartmentalized to me, but a field can overlay and interplay. I like to think of it as different levels of hot and cool air overlaying a region. The weather forecaster looks at how all of these hot and cool pockets mix together and then evaluates how they'll affect the weather. Like energy fields, hot and cool air are inseparable from one another. And, even though our bodies may seem more linear—the knee bone is connected to the leg bone, the leg bone is connected to the hip bone, as the old saying goes—the connections still apply. In reality, all of our parts make a whole: a physical, mental, emotional, and spiritual whole. It's this complete recipe that adds up to health. I cannot take out one ingredient and have it be meaningful. I trust in the flow and let go. I don't think to myself, *I must see [hear or feel] the energy fields*. However, having a possible theory of what may be happening intuitively can be helpful when explaining this process to others. More important, though, don't let labels, or how you do what you do, get in the way of your own intuiting style. When it comes right down to it, "just let go and let it flow" is exactly how I read people, and I don't let labels, explanations, or theories get in the way of intuiting.

THE BRENNAN METHOD

As I am evolving as an intuitive, I am starting to see future disease states. They look like X rays to me. I have found correlation in the work of Barbara Ann Brennan, a woman who can look at a person's aura—what she calls the Human Energy Field (HEF)—and use it to diagnose illnesses and see chakras. Once employed as a physicist by NASA, she later became a counseling professional. In this profession, she began to spontaneously see auras around her clients. She overcame doubt and skepticism through diligent practice and by testing her accuracy, developing her skill not only as a intuitive diagnostician but as a healer as well. She works in person or long-distance. In her writings, she says that she often seemed to learn something intuitively and shortly thereafter would have it validated through a book or other resource. Having to rely on the self first taught her to trust her ability. This same phenomenon has occurred in my development.

Brennan figured out the process of diagnosis and hands-on healing (sending healing energy to a client through a healer's hands) and teaches this skill to others in a highly regarded four-year program at the Barbara Brennan School of Healing. According to author Michael Talbot, "Brennan not only sees the chakras, layers and other fine structures of the human energy field with exceptional clarity, but can make startlingly accurate medical diagnoses based on what she sees."[5] In her book *Hands of Light*,[6] Brennan lays out her path of discovery in meticulous detail and suggests exercises to bring forth similar abilities in others.

I initially had difficulty understanding Brennan's methods. She sees layers on top of layers of the aura (like layers of clothing: a shirt with a sweater on top of it, with a coat on top of that). When I evaluate a person, I see things as more mixed together instead of layers on top of layers. Each of us "sees" differently, and, with time, I am feeling my way along and slowly understanding the way Brennan sees. I take the pieces that make sense to me and integrate them in my work. I have learned not to dismiss another person's methods because of initial differences. It has to be the right time and the right place for something to work. You might find the right fit with my method (the Health Intuition method), with Myss's method, with Brennan's method, a mixture of all three, someone else's, or your own. It does not matter—do what works for you.

DREAMS, TOOLS OF DIVINATION, AND SYNCHRONICITY

Aside from consciously tuning in (as discussed in chapter 13), there are other ways to obtain intuitive information, such as through dreams, tools of divination, and synchronicity.

I have met some fantastically intuitive people who do not get their information while in the waking state, but rather through dreams. Once in a while, I receive precognitive information in dreams. There are many books available on dreams, so if this topic is of interest to you, check out some of those resources. Following are the dream basics that I share with my students. The information is practical and insightful and works for most people.

Most predictive dreams occur in the morning, just before you awaken, but there are exceptions to every rule, and I'll share a personal story that illustrates this. One night I was not feeling well and went to bed very early, around 8:30 P.M. I immediately started dreaming that Barrett, one of my Newfoundland dogs, was sick and experiencing a condition called "bloat" or canine gastric volvulus. This condition happens rarely in big dogs, but it is dreaded, as it is swift and deadly. In my dream, Barrett was bloating. The dream then jumped to the next scene, where I was at work the following day, calmly doing my job. The dream was so upsetting that I awoke only an hour after going to bed. I thought, *How strange that I would be at work, because, of course, Barrett would be dead, and I would be too upset to work.* (Note the assumption here.) I got up and went out to the kitchen, where I discovered, to my horror, that Barrett really was in the very early stages of bloat. We rushed him to the vet. I was sure he would die, as I had assumed that was what my dream meant. He made it through surgery and lived. The next day, I was at work, just as I had seen in my dream.

Writing down your dreams, without making any assumptions about meanings, is key to avoiding assumptive mistakes, like my dream about Barrett. If you have trouble remembering dreams, right before you fall asleep, state to yourself the intention that you will remember your dream(s). It may take a few nights for this to work, so be patient. Set paper and pen near your bed. When you awaken, don't move. Try to recall every detail of your dream—it's like pulling a string: one event leads to another. When you feel you have every detail in your conscious mind, write it down. If you move too soon, the activity can make remembering the dream difficult. That's why I suggest you recall first, then write. Writing is important; there is something in the transcription process that leads to greater understanding of the meaning.

Interpreting your dreams can be an interesting journey. I once attended a weeklong Myss-Shealy workshop, and, after spending a lot of time in a small room, building psychic ability with thirty others who were trying to do the same, I was in a supersensitive mode. After I got home, my dreams were vibrant and symbolic and seemed to go on and on. I had never experienced anything like it. (Many of my students tell me that after the first day of attending my Health Intuition workshop, the same thing happens to them.) I now believe that my dreams were teaching me symbology. For the first time in my life, I wrote my dreams down. Many times before, it had been suggested that I journal as a therapeutic process or to get a fresh perspective on thoughts and ideas, but I resisted any kind of writing or journaling process. I was able to put this resistance aside for a few weeks and write down my dreams. At first, my dreams seemed like a foreign language, mumbo jumbo. After a few days, though, I grabbed a dream dictionary. I did not use it for literal interpretations, but rather to spark me, to teach me the language of metaphor, like brainstorming with someone to get an idea.

My intuition often speaks in metaphors. I was not even sure what the term meant when I first started intuiting. A *metaphor* is a phrase or vision that stands for something else. For example, a broken heart is not physically broken, but it is wounded on other levels. With time, the meanings of my dreams became clearer. I felt that I was being rewarded for my persistent journaling and studious interpretation. Now I usually know what the dreams mean without having to go through this process. My intuition improved a great deal during this time, because as I was coached nightly in symbology and metaphor, my intuition grew in accuracy.

I think one of the reasons we get information in dreams, instead of in our waking moments, is that it may feel safer, almost playlike. Playfulness and fun are important ingredients in intuitive success. If it's all work, you won't like it. Have fun with it. One way to do this is to use tools of divination. These are various tools that can give us intuitive insight. Most people like playing cards. As children, we are fascinated by the pretty faces of the queens, the strong images of the kings and jacks, and the vibrant reds and blacks. Tarot cards are a way to revisit that childlike wonder. But even though I have fun playing with them, I treat them with respect, and, in return, I receive solid information. In my workshops, I bring tools of divination with me. At the end of the first day, after my students and I have worked hard, it's playtime. We sit on the floor and probably look like a kindergarten class, but who cares? We're having fun. There are hundreds of tarot decks available—how do you find the one that is right for you? Just as you find anything else. Do you feel a quickening of your breath or pulse? Does it attract you? Excite your passion? Whichever one appeals to you is the right one.

There are many tools of divination. If systems are more intriguing to you, there are many to choose from. Astrology and numerology are popular, but there are dozens of others to investigate. Whatever interests you, whether mentioned here or not, is the one to try. I've noticed a gender trend in my classes: More females seem drawn to tarot, and more men like the kinesthetic aspect of working with runes or the I Ching. If you are thinking of giving a gift to someone, you might bear this in mind (remember to use your intuition to find the right one!). Traditionally, it is held that a tool of divination must be received as a gift. Don't wait—give a gift to yourself.

Some intuitives always work with tools of divination and are very good at intuiting with them. Early in my work, I took a class on using a pendulum. It worked very well. I thought: *Great! I don't have to wrestle with these doubts about my intuitive ability anymore. I can just rely on the pendulum. It will be like a third party, and I can abdicate my personal responsibility. No more doubts, no more issues, just use the pendulum!* Guess what? The pendulum stopped working for me. I then turned to my trusty tarot cards. Formerly a useful tool, they no longer gave me any information. What happened? I had unconsciously used the tools as a crutch. Anything can be a crutch, so be aware of overdependence on a person, system, or thing.

Tools of divination can help you out in tough situations where you may need intuitive information but are unable to access it because of emotional upset or some other reason. By now, you've probably guessed I'm fond of my dogs. One day, a repairman left the gate open, and they ran away. Barrett was an older dog by this time—seven—and with a heart condition. Blaize was a thirteen-week-old puppy who had lived with me for only a week. I was devastated and could not think clearly. We looked and looked, but could not find them. My intuitive impressions were tinged with emotion, and I could not get any clear impressions. In desperation, I turned to my tarot cards. I asked about the dogs' whereabouts, shuffled the deck, and pulled a card. It was the "justice" card.

Justice! There's no justice in this! I thought angrily. I shuffled again, pulled another card. Again, it was justice, and in the same position (my deck is round, so many positions are possible). Angrily, I shuffled again. My friend Seth, who had helped me look for the dogs, pointed out, "Didn't you just get the same card twice in a row? In the same position?"

"Yes," I said. "But that doesn't mean anything." Seth laughed at me as I drew a card for the third time: justice, same position. I looked up the meaning. "Everything is happening as it should, even though it doesn't appear that way. Trust, and all will be well."

With that, we opened the gate to the backyard, with the thought that maybe the dogs would find their own way home. I went to bed knowing that no matter what happened, we had given the dogs the best life they could have had. I felt filled with peace and faith, and I slept soundly despite my previously agitated state. In the morning, two very tired, bedraggled dogs were back. Once I listened, my tarot cards were able to give me the right information and helped me get through a stressful time. Use your tools of divination as you would use any tool, with respect.

As we learn to flex our intuitive "muscles" more and more, just like exercising our bodies, we may notice some changes. Perhaps you are a little sore after lifting weights or doing yard work. If you continue to labor physically, in time you will notice that what used to make you tired or out of breath is easier. Intuition works in the same way. You might find that you are capable of more as your fitness level increases. What Carl Jung called "synchronicities" (meaningful coincidences) may occur with increasing regularity. Part of this is due to increased trust in yourself. As you learn to trust in the flow, things seem to fall into place magically, and synchronicity begins to happen.

Several years ago, I was planning a trip to Connecticut with my friend Mary. We planned to stay for a few days with another friend and to visit several people, including a business contact named Bertha. As the trip drew near, my days were filled with visits to more friends and business contacts. One day, a woman named Nicole Childs called me out of the blue. Nicole explained that she knew me through a mutual friend. She asked if I might have time to visit her on this trip, at her home in Littletown, Connecticut. Unfortunately, my schedule was too tight. She said, "Well, if we're meant to cross paths, we will." I remember being impressed with the way she said it; there was an air of calmness and faith to her statement.

Meanwhile, I got a call from a woman who wanted a reading. My business is word of mouth only, so I asked how she had heard about me. She mentioned a New Age bookstore in Smallville, Connecticut. Usually, I can come up with a connection to clients, but this one stumped me. About ten minutes later, Mary telephoned, saying she had gotten a fax from my business contact, Bertha. The three of us were to meet at a halfway point between where Mary and I were staying and Bertha's home. The halfway point was at a center in Smallville, Connecticut!

A few days later, Mary and I were on our way to Connecticut. We took back roads to our meeting with Bertha and were running very late. I like to be punctual and typically would have been anxious about being late. However, I told myself, *Everything happens as it should*. I felt uncharacteristically relaxed and trusted that it all would work out. Our meeting with Bertha went well. (She, too, was running late, so there was no problem.) We finished a few minutes before 7:00 P.M. I called the New Age bookstore that had referred a client to me. They were open until 7:00! On our way to the bookstore, we saw a sign that said, "Littletown, Connecticut, 3 miles"— Nicole's hometown.

The bookstore was small, with only one man behind the counter. He was busy with a woman who could not make up her mind about which earrings went with her hair, or outfit, or something. I felt impatient. I wanted to ask the man how he knew about me. In the meanwhile, a redheaded woman walked in and began looking at the music. She seemed to know the man behind the counter, and she caught his attention before I could. I waited my turn, and finally, a few minutes before the store closed, I spoke to the man. Since I had been waiting a while, I was a little more assertive than usual.

I said, "My name is Karen Kassy, from Boulder, Colorado. I work as a health intuitive. Someone from your store sent me a client last week. I wanted to thank you and ask you if you knew who it might be. Perhaps it was Nicole Childs?" The man smiled, pointed to the redhead, and said, "That's Nicole Childs."

We hugged each other like old friends. The man behind the counter said, "This kind of thing seems to happen pretty often around here." Nicole explained that she usually worked until 7:00 P.M., but for some reason, her boss had let her off early, and she felt the need to come to the store. If it had been any later than 7:00 P.M., the store would have been closed, and we would have missed one another. If it had been any earlier, our meeting would not have occurred.

To this day, Nicole, my friend Mary, and I are amazed at the meaningful coincidences that brought us together that night. I like to think it was the trust, the belief, and the simple statement "Everything is happening as it should" that led to our wonderful experience. Now, when I'm lost, or nothing is going right, I remember that night. I remember Nicole's statement, and I relax, trust, and have faith. It always works out for the best—maybe not as I thought it would, but as it is meant to.

I take note of synchronicities and use them as a form of intuitive guidance. For example, recently I was thinking of changing doctors. I casually overheard a doctor's name in a conversation, saw her ad in the paper the next day, and had a friend tell me about her later that same day—three mentions within twenty-four hours. Before this, I had never heard of this woman, so I called and talked to the staff and visited her office. I liked what I learned, so I booked an appointment. Instead of trying doctor after doctor, I found one that worked for me the first time, thanks to the intuitive happenings of synchronicity.

Intuitive happenings may start occurring more regularly as you practice your intuition. Perhaps you'll be thinking, *I wonder what my co-worker Phil will be wearing today?* The next moment, you'll intuitively see him in a purple shirt. When you arrive at work, he's wearing a purple shirt. Or you'll be washing dishes, and all of a sudden, the answer to a long-term problem will seem to come to you out of nowhere. The next night, the same thing happens. Intuition works on a reward system: The more you pay attention and use it, the more it will come to you. Your intuition will reward you by showing you different ways of getting information.

There are as many methods of intuiting as there are people on the planet, and many tools that can aid you as well. Stay open-minded; as you change and grow, so will your methods. The way I read now is very unlike the way I started. I learned to be intuitive just as I learned to walk—one step at a time.

CHAPTER 15

Quick Practice Session

Now that you have been made aware of other people's methods of intuiting, as well as tools of divination, dreams, and ways of awareness (such as synchronicity), it's time to do another reading. You may want to incorporate some of the information I discussed in the last chapter or other information you have discovered on your own. The more you practice, the better you will become. In my weekend Health Intuition Intensive Workshops, we do a warm-up exercise followed by a group exercise, three partner readings, and a reading on yourself. That's a lot of readings—it's time for you to catch up.

If you want to read for yourself again, see if you can go a little deeper this time and get clearer information. Or how about reading for your pet?

Whomever you decide to read for, remember why we do the steps. We meditate because, when we are just starting, we need to calm our minds and reduce external stimulation so that we can see, hear, or feel the gentle presence of intuition. We invoke to protect ourselves and others, as well as to focus and ask for appropriate information. We write down the quick impressions that happen on any channel that we are comfortable receiving information through. We avoid assumptions and pay attention to the difference between intuition and emotion (like my example with the bottle cap and the letter in chapter 12). As you intuit, note that there is a quality to the "hits" and the "misses." As you receive feedback, remember how each impression "feels," a process that will guide you to be more accurate. We are energy journalists, asking *who, what, when, where, why,* and *how.* After we intuit, we shake off the energy, and we rely on our health care practitioner to make final decisions regarding our health care.

TIME TO TUNE IN

Step 1: Meditate

Spend a few quiet moments with your breath.

Step 2: Invocate

This is the invocation that I use.

_____, *please give me the information on*

(Divine source)

_____. *The truth so that*

(name and age or whatever information you have)

they can hear it and it can help them. Please let this information come through with compassion, clarity, and, if appropriate, completeness, the cause behind the cause, through my heart center.

Please do not let anything of mine (filters, biases, assumptions, etc.) interfere with the message.

I ask that none of my vital energy be used in obtaining this information.

Please send a blessing to _____.

(person for whom you are reading)

Thank you.

Step 3: Tune In

Follow the worksheet in the appendix, make your own worksheet, or use the tape recording you made. Write down your impressions. Remember to ask open-ended questions.

AS YOU FINISH

Remember to shake off the energy. Sit quietly as you come back from your intuitive state. Compare this second reading with your first one. Compare your feedback with your impressions. You may feel as though you did better—great! You may feel as though you did worse—wrong! You are learning, so any results are helpful. Remember how Henry Ford prized his intuitive "mistakes"? Learn from your hits and misses, and you'll be well on your way to intuitive improvement.

CHAPTER 16

Changes, Drawbacks, and Concerns

Synchronicity and other intuitive happenings are not the only changes you may notice as you become more intuitive. My students experience a range of emotions after the first day of my workshop. Some feel very punchy and full of energy, where normally they are mellow. Others who are usually energetic by nature feel tired. I always suggest that students watch for these shifts and be gentle with themselves. You might take a nice, relaxing bath after a hard workout of your physical self. In the same way, be kind to yourself as you grow and strengthen your intuitive self.

BODY REACTIONS

When you work out, you might notice that your muscles twitch or are sore afterward. There are other body reactions you might notice as well as you go along in your intuitive journey. Belleruth Naparstek chronicles many of these in her book *Your Sixth Sense*.[1] She interviewed more than forty intuitives and found some interesting reactions, such as changes in body temperature, lightheadedness, tingly head or feet, muscle jerks, tears, runny nose, yawns. I used to get chills after each reading. I was so cold that I had to take an hour-long hot bath to warm up. Now that I use the invocation, I am free of these kinds of body reactions. One of my students gives a slight jerk whenever she gets an impression. She is working with her invocation to mitigate this.

MY EXPERIENCES

By now, you know some of my story. I met an intuitive, researched the field, started doing readings using Myss's chakra method, developed my own system, worked with physicians to learn anatomy and to practice my skills while developing confidence and accuracy, and then began to teach. I love my work. I get to see the divine energy in each client. I feel compassion and connection to other human beings as never before. There is at least one lesson in every reading for me. It is fascinating, rewarding work.

Even if you love your work, there can be drawbacks. My biggest concern at this time is sensitivity. Being a sensitive is a double-edged sword. Think of it like a radio: As I have practiced and learned how to turn up the volume on my intuition, this turns up my volume on everything, and other sensitivities either have manifested themselves or have become magnified. I am sensitive to other people's energy. I can pick up "vibes" on people I hardly know and accurately assess their character within seconds. That is valuable, for example, in making business decisions. It saves time and trouble. The downside is that I am even more sensitive to loved ones. It is my greatest challenge not to "catch" a bad mood from my best friend. The upside? Like a buoy, if I can maintain my center by using techniques such as breath, focus, and an invocation, in the face of my loved one's emotional lows, I can stay centered in any situation. This is an area in which I have worked hard and am doing better.

Shortly after I began turning up the volume on my intuition, I began struggling with food sensitivities. Not so long ago, the wrong kinds of foods affected me on every level. My moods, my clarity, and even my skin reacted instantly and negatively if I ate something that my body deemed unacceptable. If I continued to eat inappropriate things for more than a few days, I would become very ill with a cold, flu, or some other sickness. My diet became extremely limited. I couldn't eat wheat, dairy, eggs, or sugar; nothing artificial, processed, or inorganic; even meat (aside from fish) was intolerable. Fortunately, I was able to maintain my weight, even on such a limited diet.

What did I do? I did not respond well to allergy shots. I received some help from acupuncture. I consulted my intuition, other intuitives, and health care practitioners as well, and this team is helping me get better. Through strict maintenance of a healthy diet, a lot of inner work, and the help of homeopathy, I feel more energetic and less food sensitive. Some people who are intuitive go through this phase, which I have been told is purification. Eventually, I have been reassured, I will get through it. I try to be patient, not get frustrated, and do my best. I think of purification in this way: Imagine an old sports car sitting idle; it hasn't had a tune-up or an oil change in years. All of a sudden, someone wants to use it like the sports car it was intended to be. In order to do so, the car needs to be cleaned out and given fresh oil and gas. I'm being cleaned out and purified so that I can be as efficient at handling intuition as a sports car would be at handling high-level road situations.

Some people do not experience these sensitivities, but they may manifest instead in their environment. For example, I know a few intuitives and healers who cannot live near big cities and must be in rural settings to feel balanced. If they are exposed to too many people, too much negative energy, or too much pollution, they frequently become ill.

Everything I have learned so far has been through discovery. My food sensitivities are another area I have not completely figured out but I am learning a great deal as I go along. The most important thing I have garnered from this experience is that we are not alone. This is a planet full of people, and I avail myself of practitioners, friends, and other support to get me through. When I am sick, I can feel lonely and frustrated. Through embracing the help of others and sharing my experience, I feel better.

You may be thinking, *She's a health intuitive. Why isn't she healthy?* Excellent question. Part of my original interest in this field was thinking, *Karen, if you knew what caused ill health, you could fix it and be perfectly healthy.* From time to time, when I am ill, I have to reschedule appointments. The first couple of times this happened, I was so embarrassed. My clients laughed, "Oh, you expect yourself to be perfect? It's nice to know that you're human too." They're right. I am human; I get sick. But there are differences in the way I get sick now, compared with the way I did before I learned health intuition. First and foremost, I can feel something coming on. If I'm getting a regular cold, for example (not one due to food sensitivities), I no longer have to become incapacitated in order to take time off from work and give it attention. Instead, I feel it coming on, excuse myself from work, and rest. It took time to get comfortable about leaving work when I was not in the throes of a full-blown sickness. Feeling comfortable, instead of guilty, about giving attention to your health is an important act of self-love and nurturing.

I practice a regimen that has been helpful to me in the past for colds: rest, the herb echinacea, vitamin C, and castor oil baths (an old Edgar Cayce remedy to support the immune system). If I pay attention to the writing on the wall (my intuitive knowing that I am coming down with a cold), I am able to shorten and lessen the symptoms. In the past, a cold would knock me out for anywhere from three days to a week. Now, if I take care of myself right away, it lasts anywhere from four hours to a couple of days. My colds are shorter in duration, less severe, and less frequent. Certainly this is anecdotal, not scientific, but I know others who have had similar experiences, so I believe it is worth discussing.

Not only is my health different since I started doing this work, but I now have some of the experience and patience needed to see the big picture. I realize that it takes time to heal; I may take two steps forward and one step back. Some sicknesses I get over very quickly;

others take time. The more frustrated I become when I'm sick, the worse I feel. If I relax and do not feel ashamed of needing to take time off, I seem to feel better. Be patient with yourself as you learn to listen to your body and heal. Look at the big picture: You haven't just taken a step back that day; overall, you've probably taken ten steps forward and five back. Ten steps is a lot. And don't get caught in the trap of thinking, *Because I am on a spiritual path, I shouldn't get sick.* Historically, every person on a spiritual path on this planet has eventually died, and most of them were sick first. From everyday people—like you and me—to the very public ones, we all die eventually. Mother Teresa didn't miraculously ascend into heaven without dying first; her heart failed. Does that mean she wasn't spiritual? Some spiritual leaders even use their perceived ill health to teach others. For example, the great contemporary Indian saint Ramanamaharshi had cancer. His suffering, and the way he dealt with it, proved inspirational to his followers in a way that simply talking to them could not have. He was a living example. We learn from all phases of health and living. Health takes time and attention, and who is more worthwhile to focus on than yourself? Be kind and give the gift of patience in health and healing to yourself.

My biggest struggle around an emotional issue centers on doubt, which I believe is a form of fear. In my life, I cannot remember having stage fright, not even once. Yet the first time I was assigned to do twenty readings for a doctor, I procrastinated. I was sick, I was tired, I was this, I was that. I was anything in order to avoid—consciously or unconsciously—heading forward to meet my future as an intuitive. With time, a lot of inner work, learning to value myself, and practice, I have transcended much of this fear. I keep a note on my office computer—"Doubt is negated by faith"—that helps me when fear flares up on occasion. And I have learned to herald "doubt" as a harbinger of a big step in my life. I get a little nervous before the big steps, even if I do not realize their future impact.

For example, in order to complete my master's degree, I had to write the thesis. This last step was all that was needed to obtain the degree. Although I am usually organized and on time, I could not get started. At the same time, I was not getting any requests for readings. Every day, I went to the post office, and my box was empty. In a bit of synchronicity, I received the intuitive message "Start writing your thesis, and the readings will come." The day I started my thesis, there were seven requests for readings in my post office box. Now that I know that my doubts and fears are calling my attention to meaningful issues, I can look them full in the face—sometimes with the aid of a friend and always with the help of my intuition—and transcend them.

THE BUSINESS SIDE OF HEALTH INTUITION

In my workshop, I spend a little time going over what it's like to do this work professionally. Not everyone wants to do it for a living. In my case, it took time to build a client base. I decided not to advertise as a way of testing myself—again, overcoming doubt about how good my ability was. I reasoned that if my readings were accurate, people would refer their friends to me. I was right; however, it takes time to build a business using only word of mouth.

This field is uncharted territory legally. The attorneys I work with tell me they cannot find any laws on the books governing what I do; health/medical intuition is a gray area in the legal realm. There is a danger that I could be accused of practicing medicine without a license. I try to avoid the appearance of doing so: I require clients to get their doctor's approval to consult with me, and I insist that people check with their health care practitioners before making any decisions about their health. I try to practice with integrity.

The field is becoming more crowded, and you may have noticed that I call myself a *health intuitive* instead of the more popular term *medical intuitive*. When something becomes popular, it attracts both positive and negative elements. One of the reasons I came up with this term and service marked it (Health Intuitive^{sm}) is to differentiate myself from others who may not be as accurate or who may not practice with professional standards. While some people practicing under other labels for this work are accurate and practice with integrity, others do not. I want to make sure the term *health intuitive* stands for only that work which is accurate and is practiced with integrity. I believe this is a profession of the future. In order to survive, it will have to be organized, or it will be legislated out of existence. I would someday like to have an International Society of Health Intuitives. I want us to be recognized as an organized, practiced, accurate group that works with a code of ethics to help people with their health. With a group of talented, skillful professionals, we can move forward and legitimize health intuition as a profession or a skill. It is a wonderful adjunct, not a substitute, for medical care. People have been using intuition in one form or another to treat illness for thousands of years. I would like to see that continue.

LOOKING FOR AN INTUITIVE

What qualities should you look for in a good intuitive? There are many, but three seem especially important. First, find one with a communication style that works for you. One of my clients, Patrice, came to me after she spent $500 for a half-hour reading with someone else ($350 for the reading and $150 for the intuitive's line of vitamin supplements). When people are sick, they are vulnerable. Patrice believed that if she paid a lot, she would get a lot. She believed in that old adage "You get what you pay for." Unfortunately for her, what she received was a confusing reading, an audiotape she could not hear, and a follow-up printout that contradicted what the intuitive had originally told her. Patrice called back for clarification, but was told that the intuitive was too busy to speak to her.

Patrice might have benefited from talking to another client of mine, Roland. Roland met a psychic who initially gave him a free and accurate reading. The next time he went to her, it cost $50; the next time, $200; the next time, $450; and so on. Finally he came to me, with a note he had received from the psychic. It said, "Send $2,800 by Thursday, or a piece of your soul that is missing will be gone forever." (I have never heard of "soul snatching" and consulted with colleagues who agreed that it sounded like a ruse.) Roland said, "I think I'm being taken advantage of." If you think you are being taken advantage of, you probably are. Not everyone who has intuition also possesses integrity.

Early in my development as a health intuitive, I met one of the most accurate intuitives I have ever known. Frank was incredible. He intuitively knew names, dates, everything. He read for me (and my roommate) and encouraged me on my path. I felt fortunate to have met him. A few weeks after meeting Frank, bizarre things started happening to me. I'm not one of those intuitives who experiences bumps in the night, but all of a sudden, in the middle of the night, lights started turning on and off in my home, the computer and printer started going, and the bed would shake. I would have thought I was going insane if my roommate had not been there to witness everything. This went on for several weeks. We turned to Frank, who had built our trust through months of accurate readings. Frank told us that we were possessed by "entity energy" (his terminology for an unearthly being implanting itself in my roommate and me). Since nothing like this had ever happened before and I had no resources or experience to rely on, I believed him. He suggested a few remedies, but nothing worked. I became afraid to go to sleep or to venture outside after dark. I relied on Frank more and more.

One weekend, a man I deeply respect came to town. Seamus is a trained shaman and a highly regarded healer. Despite his work in the paranormal, he invariably puts a "normal" spin on everything and is very down-to-earth. I always feel comfortable around him. I explained to him over the phone that the furniture was shaking, lights were turning on and off, and nothing was working to bring my home back to its formerly peaceful state. A few days later, he came over. He went into the bedroom, burned some sage, chanted, and did some shamanic work for five minutes.

"You had a couple of spirits who were attracted to your brightening energy. I helped them cross over," Seamus said. In many spiritual traditions, there is a limbo state where souls who have died but not reached their destination may need help in reaching it. This is what Seamus calls "crossing over."

When I told Seamus about my experiences with Frank, he was quiet for a moment. Then he said, "Be careful what you give your attention to." He did not chastise me or deride Frank. Instead, he offered reassurances and told me I was not contaminated with entity energy. Seamus did not tell me what to do; he left it up to me to make my own choices. As a result, I felt empowered when he left.

A few days later, Frank inquired about the paranormal activity in my home. Without really thinking, I said, "Oh, I called in a shaman. He took care of it. Everything's fine." It was, but Frank wasn't. He was furious. I thought he would be happy that my problems were over; instead, he was upset and offended. In retrospect, I can see what had happened. I was giving him my energy, my attention, my power. Frank had me in a state of fear, turning to him constantly. After I asked Seamus for help, and he encouraged me to rely on myself, I became re-empowered, and the bond was broken. Frank grew increasingly agitated, said some inappropriate things, and was out of my life.

I later learned that Frank had been using his intuitive skills to manipulate other young women. He didn't seem to work with men or older women. "Entity energy" seemed to be a ploy he used to meet young women. I heard about this behavior from several different sources, and the stories were all the same. Nothing like this had happened before I met Frank, and no more problems have occurred since I have broken off all contact with him.

Frank was one of my greatest teachers. He is an incredibly intuitive person who uses his power to induce fear in others. At a Foundation of Shamanic Studies workshop, I asked shaman and teacher Sandra Ingerman about this type of person. She said, "There is an old-fashioned name for an intuitive or a healer using fear to manipulate others: *sorcery*." *Sorcery* is a term that has been around for thousands of years. I doubt that Frank was a trained sorcerer, but he certainly espoused the shadow side of intuitive work, whether intentional or not. I mentioned earlier that high prices are not necessarily the sign of an accurate intuitive. The converse is true, as well: Frank's readings were free.

How can you verify an intuitive's reputation for integrity and accuracy? When you call to set up the appointment, ask for references. If the intuitive becomes upset or refuses, consider looking elsewhere. I have a letter of recommendation from a physician stating that my accuracy is 80 to 90 percent. Another health care practitioner whom I can use as a reference believes that my accuracy is even higher— closer to 98 percent. However, references are seldom requested of me, because most of my clients are sent to me by a trusted friend or health care practitioner (which can also be a good way to find other people who do this work).

BECOMING A PROFESSIONAL

Not everyone is cut out to be a health intuitive. Occasionally, I will get a call from someone who is just starting out. He or she is upset at the prospect of giving inaccurate information to a client. This is a valid concern. That is why I advocate practicing with health care practitioners to hone your craft first. Dr. C. Norman Shealy suggests that an intuitive needs to be at least 75 percent accurate.[2] Find out if you are accurate enough to work as a professional intuitive.

If you like it, are good at it, and feel that, at the end of every reading, you can go back to your daily life without getting caught up in your client's life, it *may* be for you. On the other hand, if you are uncomfortable with the legal risks, can't let go, and don't seem to have the skill or a level of ease with the work, don't do it.

CHAPTER 17

Practice

By now, you're probably tired of hearing the "p-word," but practice is the key to improving your intuitive abilities. You might be thinking about practicing on other people. In my weekend workshops, we do an everyday intuition exercise on decision making (to warm up), a group intuition exercise, and then we partner with someone else to practice reading a stranger (someone else taking the class who you don't know). Often, people come to a workshop with their friends, but I encourage them to try working with someone they do not know. Our skeptical left brain can think of many ways to explain away intuition, and it will have an easier time of it if you are reading a friend ("Oh, but I knew that already"). With a stranger, the hits you get are much harder to deny, because there is no way you could have known any facts about that person. Also, it can get a little sticky practicing on your friends. When I first started out, I lost two friends because they thought what I was doing was too intrusive, even though I had their permission.

During the Introduction to Health Intuition Weekend Intensive, we partner three times. Just as you did in the reading for yourself, we follow the three-step process: meditate, invocate, tune in (and write down). When finished, each partner shakes off the energy and receives feedback. I guide the first two readings of the weekend. For the last reading, I lead the meditation and invocation, and then each person does the exercise in his or her own way. There are many creative ways to read someone. Some of my students follow my pattern: a bottom-to-top body scan using the body worksheet. Others prefer to go top to bottom. I have seen students draw a body and write in their impressions or draw pictures of what they see, hear, or feel. Some use the chakra system. Once in a while, instead of sitting and receiving the information, someone will use their hands to scan the energy of the body. The variations are endless, and all of them are perfect because they suit the individual doing the reading.

Only once in all the years I have been teaching has there been a problem. On the last exercise, a set of partners left the room to do a reading on each other before I did the meditation and invocation. Both ended up angry. When I asked how they did the reading, they admitted that they did not do the invocation and could see that the invocation would have kept them out of trouble. Their intuition was not focused on "the truth so that they can hear it and it can help them," and they did not protect themselves. As a result, each gave a reading that was too direct and painful for the other to hear, and both ended up hurt. I had thoroughly explained the purpose of the invocation during the workshop. This pair went a little too fast and forgot to set the foundation for their work. Remember to invocate and meditate; both are a great help.

PRACTICING ON OTHER PEOPLE

If you want to practice your intuition on other people, first consider any laws in your area. For example, I am an ordained minister. I initially became a minister because a colleague told me that it gave me some protection under the law. Later, I asked my attorneys, who told me you can be sued anywhere, for anything, even walking across someone's lawn. It does not matter if the advice is free, given as a minister, or charged for, you can still be sued. When I lived in

Colorado, my status as a minister gave me the right to protect the confidentiality of my clients in court, which is very important to me. Also, some clients feel more comfortable speaking with someone who is in the role of spiritual counselor. But I am not a lawyer, so please seek good legal advice before you read for others.

A simple and legal way to practice your health intuition skills is to read the obituaries. I know it seems morbid, but it's a great way to get immediate feedback. The newspaper lists the name and age of the deceased. Cover up the other details of the article with your hand and intuit. Then compare your impressions with what is written. What did this person do for a living? What are some of the details of his or her life? Was the person married? Divorced? Did he or she have children? A less-morbid practice would be to use *Who's Who*, which contains detailed biographies of many famous people. At least once a year, but usually more often, *People* magazine seems to devote a whole issue to public figures who are experiencing illnesses. Certainly, it is sad to know that someone is ill, but since this information is public and published with the cooperation of those featured, why not practice with it? It seems that nearly every issue has one interview with a famous person who is sharing the details of his or her life and sickness. Try intuiting before you read the article.

MORE WAYS TO PRACTICE

Everyday intuition is easily practiced. There are a hundred ways, each day, to do so. I have mentioned many throughout the book, but to recap a few: guess how much your groceries or gas will be, what time it is, which way you should go for the best parking place or the quickest route; or who's on the phone. Again, Sonia Choquette's book *The Psychic Pathway* is a wonderful resource for practice.

How about incorporating intuition into your business? Aside from the applications of this book to a health care practice (see pages 207–211), these techniques can also be used in other professions. I know a real estate agent who takes people out *one* time and then knows exactly what type of house is perfect for them. She explains, "I show my client a bunch of houses. From watching his or her reaction and response, I have a good idea about what type of house is right for them." She then incorporates her intuition and chooses from hundreds of listings to take her client to just one house. Nearly every time, that one house is the perfect home. The client and agent save time, money, and frustration, thanks to intuition.

OTHER BENEFITS

As your intuition grows, you will notice an interesting phenomenon: You begin to recognize people by the energy they give off instead of by their appearance. Have you ever been introduced to someone you've never met before, but you cannot shake the feeling that he or she is familiar? Later, you realize that Randy reminds you of your acquaintance Joe. He looks nothing like Joe, talks nothing like Joe, but he's a Joe. Learn to pay attention to these energy similarities. For example, chances are that Randy, like Joe, has a penchant for not showing up on Saturdays to help out as promised, borrowing money without paying it back, and leaving town for weeks at a time. Next time, save yourself some trouble. Watch for clues to similarities of behavior and exercise caution before becoming involved. More often than not, your energy recognition and hunches will pan out.

On the flip side, Jonah is a new acquaintance, but you feel as though you have known him forever. He reminds you so much of your old friend Linus that it's as if you are spending time with the same person. Consider trusting this energy hunch as well. Life is short, and trust is a rare commodity. We are so separated, often by fear, from our fellow humans. With television, the Internet, commutes to work, and busy lives, there is seldom time to spend with our neighbors, let alone friends and family. Use intuition as a way to connect with others.

Encourage intuition in your children. So many of them express it bountifully, yet it is unsupported, shut down, or misunderstood. Judith Orloff, a psychiatrist and clairvoyant, spent a good deal of her life trying to overcome guilt and anxiety over her childhood intuitive experiences. Her book *Second Sight*[1] tells how she eventually overcame the guilt and anxiety, and it serves as a lesson for all of us who are in a position to mentor others. The trust issues many adults deal with begin in childhood. What is one of the first things you are taught? "Don't talk to strangers." Yet what do you do if you are lost or in trouble? My niece is three years old. I hope that I can encourage her parents to instill in her enough reliance on her own good instincts so that she faces the world with common sense and trust instead of an overabundance of fears. If we are afraid to connect with others—and our children are too—how do we expect to work together to solve our problems and the uncertainties that face our planet? Learn to listen to yourself and teach and encourage that trust in others. With intuition in place, both you and your loved ones can live a life of more fulfilling relationships based on trust, not fear.

HOW INTUITION IS VIEWED

For every perceived positive, there is a shadow side: something we may judge as bad or negative or with which we are uncomfortable. As you become more intuitive, you may experience people who criticize your ability or, in the extreme case, treat you as if you are evil. These are obstacles to overcome in integrating intuitive practice into your daily life. Needing credit for your intuition from anyone but yourself is a sure road to burnout and disappointment.

A friend of mine has a hot tub. When he first got it, he thought that everyone would want to come over. He was deeply disappointed that only a handful of friends shared his enthusiasm. Some people didn't like the heat, others didn't want to be seen in their swimsuits, some were uncomfortable with the intimacy aspect, and so on. Part of the reason he bought the tub in the first place was so that people would spend more time with him. Eventually, he let go of his investment in the outcome and enjoyed the therapeutic benefits of the tub himself. Once he was less sensitive to others not liking the tub, several friends began to use it.

Intuitive validation is similar. When you feel special because you *are* special, not because you know something private about someone else and want him or her to acknowledge you, that is when people are most receptive. Intuition is not a road to popularity, fame, power over others, or an inflated sense of self-importance. I believe it works poorly under these conditions (even though Frank may have used his intuition to manipulate others, he was eventually found out and rejected). If you want to improve your intuition and its receptivity by others, clear your need for approval from other people. You can do this through inner work or the aid of other resources like books, tapes, workshops, or counseling sessions. Then intuition can flow purely into you, regardless of outcome.

The movie *Phenomenon* showed how people may react to someone with special intuitive or other paranormal abilities. There are many ways to avoid or mitigate negative reactions. Ask before offering intuitive insights. Use your intuition to see if it is appropriate to peek at someone or to share impressions. Use benign terms such as *dream, hunch, insight,* and *gut feeling.* Steer clear of hot-button terms like *psychic* or *fortune-telling.* Even the gentler word *intuition* can set some people off. If you encounter someone who believes that intuition is against the Christian religion, consider referring them to

1 Corinthians 12: 4–11, Gifts of the Spirit:

> Now there are varieties of gifts, but the same Spirit; and there are varieties of service, but the same Lord; and there are varieties of working, but it is the same God who inspires them all in every one. To each is given the manifestation of the Spirit for the common good. To one is given through the Spirit the utterance of wisdom, and to another the utterance of knowledge according to the same Spirit, to another faith by the same Spirit, to another gifts of healing by the one Spirit, to another the working of miracles, to another prophecy, to another the ability to distinguish between spirits, to another various kinds of tongues, to another the interpretation of tongues. All these are inspired by one and the same Spirit, who apportions to each one individually as he wills.

Realize that no matter what you do, some people will not be happy. Be content within yourself and practice your intuition with honesty, integrity, and diplomacy. Incorporate it as you would any other talent into your life.

INCORPORATING INTUITION IN A HEALTH CARE PRACTICE

Intuition is a wonderful adjunct to any health care practice. It can give insights and perspectives that are not always readily available. If you work with a client's or patient's whole self—physical, mental, emotional, and spiritual—the healing can be more complete. Intuition does not seem to interfere with any healing systems;

rather, it synthesizes, and it can save time.

If you are a health care practitioner, you can easily add intuition to your practice. I have seen an entire clinic of practitioners work as a team to intuit on a client, each adding his or her own area of expertise to come up with a total treatment plan for the whole client. Whether you are part of a group or an individual practitioner, you can use intuition to give you new insights. Many of my students have augmented their healing practices with intuition. To give you an idea of how wide-ranging this practice is, here is a list of some types of practitioners who have taken my health intuition workshops: acupuncturists, bodyworkers, doctors of osteopathy, hands-on healers, healing touch practitioners, herbalists, massage therapists, medical doctors, nursing professionals, nutritionists, psychiatrists, psychologists, psychotherapists, reiki practitioners, shamans, and therapeutic touch practitioners. Their commonly held viewpoint: "If something works, and it helps my clients and patients, I will use it."

How do these healers incorporate health intuition? Some take a few minutes to tune in to clients before each appointment; some intuit during sessions. Many share with their clients what they are doing; others keep their intuitive practice to themselves. All verify their intuitive feelings before acting on them, checking their common sense and knowledge base before treatment. They realize that intuition is not a substitute for medical care.

It was my privilege to do a reading for Veronica, who was about to embark on her life's purpose as a healer. Learning about how she needed to shift some of her attitudes provides valuable information for health care professionals. It will also serve people who want to improve their relationship with others. The following are excerpts from her reading:

> Your healing priorities can take many forms. Do not
> get caught up in labels or jockey for position in your

profession. Work on the few issues listed below to finish clearing yourself as much as possible, so the purity of light and love that is to come through you can and does. Just a few things: This will not be a physical reading per se, but more of a spiritual one. It is what you need to do to prepare.

Let go of the judgment and the judging mind. "That's true of me too" must become your mantra. Do not misjudge those who are blind, stone deaf, and like lepers who can no longer feel. You, as a wise crone woman, offer them a vision of beauty and a way to be led and follow until they can stand up straight, cast off their beggar's robes and leper colonies, and see and feel the way. They chose the slow path for learning so that they could learn best and most deeply. You've been there. Your patience with them is appreciated, but your judgment is not. Stop looking over them: instead, look onto them with love and patience and kindness, for they need all your help and understanding on a spiritual, emotional, mental, and physical level. You work with the weak, but you both become strong.

Needling doubt in your mind is another powerful issue. The doubting mind *(What should I do? What if they think I'm a wacko?)* is in the way. Realize that it is your faith, your divine connection, that enables you to perform these miracles. Go with faith and banish the doubting mind forever.

Guilt, when there is not enough of you to go around and help someone. Realize that you can take on only so many, do so much, and that the others you can't get to have a more appropriate time, place, individual, and lesson waiting for them elsewhere—you are not the one for them, and they are not the one for you.

And last, please make sure you take ultimate physical care of your health, especially your feet, as you face a challenging road ahead. Optimal physical health—supported by correct diet, exercise, and mental attitude and strengthening (meditation, chi kung, etc.)—will be of great help to you.

Stay true to your integrity and honesty. Ask your divine connection or intuition when you are unsure which way to go and what to do, then sit back and wait. It will come clearly to you.

Veronica, blessed healer, collect and correct these few issues and you will be well on your way to the path that lies ahead. Bless you for the undertaking and your strength of character and faith. They will hold you in good stead as you walk the rocky and rough-hewn path of beauty, love, healing, love, compassion, and love. Bless you.

The excerpts from Veronica's reading point out some important mental, emotional, and spiritual aspects to the healing journey. I have found in my own life that the key word is *balance*. I spend a lot of time in my head intuiting, writing, and preparing materials for teaching. What balances me? Using my whole body, not just my head. Last year, I was given the gift of a season pass at a downhill ski resort. Initially, I was reluctant to take time away from my clients; however, I wanted to honor the gift-giver by using the pass. After the first day on the slopes, I felt refreshed, renewed. My intuitive readings seemed to improve in accuracy and ease. This trend seemed to hold if I got up on the slopes at least every two weeks. When I did not go skiing, the readings seemed harder to do, more challenging. I also have incorporated other exercise into my life, such as stretching and breathing and walking. When I practice these consistently and regularly, everything, including my intuition, seems to flow. If I consciously keep my meditation time (relaxation and quiet mind) at a consistent level, I find the same flowing effect.

My massage therapist, Ponchita, whom I used to see twice a year, asked me an important question one day: "Karen, you spend so much time giving; is there ever a time when you are just receiving? Without having to give?"

Think of how that might apply in your own life. Like me, you may find that you cannot come up with any time where you just receive. As a result, when I am busy, I make sure that I take time out for a massage about once a month. Again, it seems to improve the flow of my intuition. Find what balancing strategies work for you, and your intuition will benefit as well.

CHAPTER 18

Another Quick Practice

Time to refresh your skills. Make intuition a practice—a good habit—and it will flow more easily to you. If you want to read for yourself again, by all means, continue to develop that relationship. In my workshops, I suggest that people commit to reading themselves at least the first day of every month. Some students do it weekly, some daily. Eventually, you find that your self communicates with you whenever necessary.

If you read for your pet last time, you could read for another animal or deepen your intuitive relationship with the first pet. Or following some of my examples from the last chapter, how about intuitively reading some people listed in the obituaries or *Who's Who?* If you have decided that it is legal and safe for you to practice with a partner or on a friend, you can follow the same process.

Meditate, invocate, and tune in. Write down the quick impressions that happen on the audio, visual, or kinesthetic levels. Avoid assumptions and pay attention to the difference between intuition and emotion. Give your left brain the energy journalist task, asking the five Ws and the one H. Look into all levels. When you intuit about feet, for example, look beyond physical information; work to discern emotional, mental, and spiritual components. Be practical—are there any intuitive suggestions for the person (or animal) you are reading to pursue a shift? After you intuit, shake off the energy. Remind the person you are reading for to consult with his or her health care practitioner before making any changes.

TIME TO TUNE IN

Step 1: Meditate

Spend a few quiet moments with your breath.

Step 2: Invocate

_____, *please give me the information on*
(Divine source)

_____. *The truth so that*
(name and age or whatever information you have)

*they can hear it and it can help them. Please let this infor-
mation come through with compassion, clarity, and, if
appropriate, completeness, the cause behind the cause,
through my heart center.*

*Please do not let anything of mine (filters, biases, assump-
tions, etc.) interfere with the message.*

*I ask that none of my vital energy be used in obtaining this
information.*

Please send a blessing to _____.
(person for whom you are reading)

Thank you.

Step 3: Tune In

Follow the body worksheet in the appendix, a worksheet of your own
design, or the tape recording you made. Write down your impressions. Remember to ask open-ended questions.

AS YOU FINISH

Remember to shake off the energy. Sit quietly as you come back from your intuitive state. How did this third reading feel compared with the other two? If you are doing this with a partner or on someone else, compare the feedback with your impressions. Remember, you are just starting out, practicing—be patient with yourself and rejoice that you are learning something new.

CHAPTER 19

A Human Being
Instead of a Human Doing

Do, do, do. It seems that most of my clients are so active that they cannot comfortably relax and just be. Relaxation can help us attain balance. Most of us need to work toward balance, and when it is attained, life feels more effortless. Balance was not a major component of my "former life." Ambitiously scratching my way to the top as a corporate executive—fighting, planning, scheming, manipulating—I'd never once experienced letting life's plans unfold.

Caroline Myss has a wonderful saying: "I thank the gods for giving me no ambition and tons of talent for something I have no interest in." Certainly, I quickly became interested in health intuition after my first meeting with an intuitive on that fateful day, but I did not pursue it. Nearly a year later, I took three months off work and, without consciously realizing it, practiced *being* instead of *doing*. For once, I cultivated trust and faith that everything was working out. I tried to stay in the present moment, knowing that whatever future was coming to me would come in its own time and way.

Once my path was somewhat clear, I cooperated. I researched, learned, practiced, and interned with health care professionals to become a competent intuitive. I worked hard to become a teacher and public speaker, taking every ounce of constructive criticism and incorporating it into my workshops and talks. And when the universe sent me literally dozens of individuals asking, "When's your book coming out?" I wrote one.

Being a teacher was the last thing on my list. I was more than uninterested; I was *dis*interested. Looking back, I can see that a divine plan was set up for me. Unfortunately, I was 100 percent busy being a human doing, with no balance of being, so at the time I couldn't see the plan. I worked for not one but two companies that promoted public speakers. Listening to hundreds of professional speakers, I realized how hard it is to be a good teacher. I decided it was something I *never* wanted to do. But every job I've ever had—in publishing, in business, in writing, in editing, in running a business—has set me up for this career. Many relationships have come back to me, again and again, to play a role in the success and development of this livelihood. For example, my best friend was a star on the speech and debate team in high school and majored in public speaking in college. He helped coach me when I first started out, giving up weekend after weekend to attend every one of my first workshops.

Once I slowed down, balanced, and learned to listen to myself through intuition, it all came into play. I now have the privilege of living a delicious life that I feel complete congruence with. I love being a health intuitive, teaching and reading for people. I have found myself, and my purpose, by listening within.

I have spoken to many people who have had similar experiences; they feel awe and a certain calmness about how it all unfolded for them. You can encourage the process in your life. Using your intuition, tune in to yourself. Work to develop the inner qualities that resonate integrity, honesty, or whatever attracts you to right action. Live your life congruently. Cultivate relationships with others and yourself. Walk your talk. And, through meditative practice, stay open to the future, but stay in the now. Have faith that everything is turning out as it is meant to, and then watch while it unfolds. As Yogananda says, "Bring into play the almighty power that is within you, so that on the stage of life you can fulfill your destined role."[1]

Your purpose may turn out to be something totally different than you would ever have expected, as in my case, but looking back, you'll see that it is perfection in every sense. It is so *me*; it is so *you*. Await and cooperate. The gift of you, of your livelihood expressing you, will then be able to happen.

PUTTING IT ALL TOGETHER

Learning takes time. How much? Maybe a lifetime. It doesn't matter. Because as you go along and incorporate the lessons, it all comes together and flows. There are ups and downs, but, like that buoy, you ride the storms and the gentle breezes in a centered manner.

A friend of mine, Justine, called me as I was finishing this book to tell me a wonderful story. I loved it so much—and found that it illustrates principles from both sections of this book so well—that I thought I would share it.

Justine began her professional career as a waitress. Through her work, she became friendly with a customer who owned a fledgling company whose primary purpose was to disseminate spiritual wisdom. Eventually, she went to work for him and trained as a graphic artist. She worked there for several years and developed strong relationships with co-workers and key people in the company. The hours were long and the pay was low. She learned a lot about graphic arts, and her own emotional, mental, and spiritual life, but eventually it was time to move on. She recognized the writing on the wall, and she resigned. She left the company on excellent terms with the people who worked there and took a break.

Five months later, she found another job, at twice the pay and with a greater opportunity to learn and grow. She applied herself and learned how to design Web pages for the Internet, how to create computer games, and how to manage people—she even learned a little marketing. As the years went by, her job grew less challenging and no longer offered opportunities to acquire new skills and knowledge. Again, she felt intuitive hints that it was time to go. She began to tie up loose ends, finish projects, and put everything in order. Justine needed only one more month to set up a financial cushion before she resigned. She held no anger toward the people of the company; she enjoyed working with them very much. Justine knew that it was the work that no longer excited her passion or held great meaning. She did not feel guilty for leaving a "good job with good pay." She was unafraid of what the future held, knowing that it was simply time to move on. She had enough faith in herself and in the divine plan that she knew she would be fine. Her attitude remained upbeat, and none of her co-workers had an inkling she was planning to leave. She did not speak behind others' backs or blame them for her unhappiness. She knew it was time for the next phase of her life.

One month before her planned resignation, she was laid off. As she explained this part of the story to me, she said: "I was in shock. I had no idea this was coming. At first, my boss gave me a huge project with impossible deadlines. Two days later, it was made to seem as if I was not doing my job. It was almost as if he was trying to fire me. This happened in the space of only a few days. I was laid off. I felt hurt, but philosophical. After all, I was planning to leave soon, anyway."

A few weeks after she first told me this story, I spoke to her, and she gave me this update:

"The most amazing thing has happened! I didn't know what I wanted to do or what I would be doing. My co-workers felt so bad about the way they perceived I had been treated that, unbeknownst to me, they started calling everyone they knew, asking if there was any work for me. I've been getting so many calls! I don't even have a computer yet—I'm getting one tomorrow. I don't even have business cards, and I've already landed a terrific freelance job with fabulous money! Looking back on it, my boss handled the situation badly. But who wouldn't? It's not easy to lay someone off. My co-workers have been calling and pouring their hearts out to me. I listen, but I don't take it on. I don't have bad feelings, and there's no bitterness. Even my financial situation has worked out, because I was given a severance that more than made up for my shortfall."

Justine is not an old woman. She works hard on herself and has been able to attain this kind of compassion and life-flow at the ripe old age of thirty-three. It is possible. Age is not a barrier nor a prerequisite. The only two requirements are intention and practice, practice, practice.

THE FOUR THINGS YOU CAN DO
FOR EACH LEVEL OF BEING

I have mentioned the physical, mental, emotional, and spiritual levels many times in this book. To provide you with a simple foundation of priorities from which to work, I've chosen one important aspect for each of the four levels. From this foundation, you can build according to your individual needs, adding the things you need to work on. The more you intuit, the more aware you will become of the areas you need to work on in yourself. You will then begin to live your life more congruently with your spirit or true purpose. Thus, while you are helping yourself, you can also help others. The more you work on yourself, the better the quality of your intuition. And as you practice your intuitive skills and learn to listen to yourself, you become a better person.

Physical

The most important aspect of this level is a combination of nutrition and exercise. Nutrition is the foundation of your physical body. If you want your house (body) to withstand the elements, you need to build it out of the best materials available. Part two of this formula is moderate and consistent exercise. Good nutrition and exercise are the most powerful physical elements you can integrate to aid your health.

Mental

Quiet the mind. We think so much. Our minds need a break or a vacation. If possible, meditate, contemplate, or quiet the mind at the same time each day (to establish a consistent practice). You'll find that your thinking, your intuition, and your life in general will flow more clearly and easily.

Emotional

Release. Seeing patterns that no longer serve you (those that became apparent as you read section 1 of this book) and working to transcend, shift, and release them clears you. As you become more present, with less clutter (issues) in your life, you are better able to release past situations through forgiveness. You can give yourself the love you deserve, as you have released and forgiven yourself.

Spiritual

Cultivate the divine connection. You are never alone, and you will have direct access to an unlimited flow of divine, untainted, and limitless energy.

These four areas, and the accompanying suggestions, work in tandem with each other to create improved health and well-being. These are simple guidelines, easy to remember. Start today to integrate them into your life. Once you have begun, you will notice you are feeling better in many ways. They add up to one key word: *balance*. Determine where you are out of whack and work to re-balance. Check every aspect of your life—attitudes, work, relationships, thinking patterns, habits, and so on. Balance is the key to making your dream life a reality. Just hold the intention and practice, practice, practice.

In the future, I would like to expand my intuitive awareness to other fields, in addition to health, life purpose, and business. I need to remember that I will not instantly be 80 to 90 percent accurate when I apply intuition to other areas of interest. I will start as a beginner. Eventually, I also want to do more work with animals. I've started slowly, but constantly have to remind my doubting self that it takes practice to improve.

If you find in your intuitive practice that an exercise does not work for you or that your impressions seem to be inaccurate, do a little detective work. Is it your impressions that are wrong or your interpretation? Are you meant to get information about a certain subject or person, or is that not your path? Most important, be gentle with yourself, take baby steps, set the intention, practice, and, with time, you will know. The greatest teachers in the world are experience and application. Take whatever you have read in this book that resonates for you, and teachings from other sources and from your own life. Integrate, apply, experience. Then, and only then, will you shift and grow into the intuitive being you are, who listens to your inner knowing, considers carefully, and acts in your best interest. The result? A life that flows and is full of passion, meaning, improved health, and greater well-being.